LOSS
to BOSS

Randy,
Wishing you abundant
joy and success!

Warm wishes, 12/21

LOSS to BOSS

Frank DeMaio

Great Point Publishing
Gloversville, NY

Loss to Boss: How to Find a Job
Frank DeMaio

Cover Design By: Kara DeMaio
Book design by: Great Point Publishing LLC

To order additional copies of this title, contact your favorite local bookstore or visit *www.greatpointpublishing.com*

Paperback ISBN: 978-1-955334-06-8

Hardcover ISBN: 978-1-955334-13-6

Printed in the United States of America

Published by: **Great Point Publishing, LLC.**
                      Gloversville, NY

This Book is Dedicated To

My Wife Kelli, and Our Sons Luca and Frankie

for always supporting my dreams and ambitions, picking me up
when I need it most, and showing me unconditional love.

I love you more than I can express.

TABLE OF CONTENTS

Foreword

My name is Dr. Tom Denham, and it is an honor to write the Foreword to Frank's book <u>Loss to Boss</u>. As a practicing Career Counselor for over 30 years, I have seen my fair share of clients go through the trauma of job loss. It's not pretty. It can be devastating for many. Job loss can happen to anyone, and no field is immune. Remember any feelings you have are perfectly normal. This is not the end, but merely a new chapter for you. Trust the process.

What I have learned is that the hard work of the job search takes place in between the sessions. When I work with clients, I often suggest that they find a book on career development that speaks to them when we are not together in the private practice. I think you will find Frank's book a guide and companion as you navigate your unique transition.

Quickly, he sets an empathic tone with readers by bringing his own real life job loss story to the table. The author is able to make that important and emotional connection with the reader. His goal is to help others overcome job loss based on his own setback and subsequent comeback. In addition, the book's interviews with others who have been downsized are helpful. You may just find you have some similarities in your own loss.

The book touches on a variety of topics. I particularly like how he first addresses the emotional and psychological impact of job loss instead of just going right to job search strategies. The book talks about the value in self-assessment which is the first stage of the career development process. I especially like that he advocates for taking self-assessment inventories and provides a list of options. Inventorying your values, interests, personality traits and skills is essential to creating a match with jobs that are best fits for you. Throughout the book there are exercises, worksheets, and opportunities to take notes which I strongly advocate as a practitioner. The book then moves into exploring your options.

After careful assessment and exploration, the reader will learn some of the mechanics of the job search. This includes resume, cover letters and references. The book helps you understand Applicant Tracking Systems (ATS) as part of the hiring process. This resource also discusses job search techniques and marketing. As well as the most important; being networking. The three rules of the job search are networking, networking, networking. Frank also includes several personal stories of others, including one that highlights the importance of reaching out to others for help in the search.

Chapter 8 deals with the most neglected part of the job search - preparing for interviews. The three rules of interviewing are practice, practice, practice. The book also highlights the importance of having a well-crafted and rehearsed Elevator Speech.

This book has an important message – you can overcome job loss! I think you will find the information in this book to be both informative and instructional.

Dr. Tom Denham
Career Counselor
Careers In Transition LLC
Albany, NY
www.careersintransitionllc.com

Chapter 1

Shocked

I was in the same shoes you are in right now.

My position and department, due to a reorganization, was ultimately eliminated.

I remember exactly what happened and how I found out. I was scheduled for a one-on-one meeting with my new "manager" as a meet and greet due to a recent reorganization. At the time I had been with my employer for over a decade.

I was obviously unnerved, as this was the first time I was going to meet them. As such you are not always sure what their personality might be or how you are going to get along with them, what their expectations are going to be and what type of leadership style they may have. Are they laissez-faire, autocratic, authoritative, micromanager, etc.? How do those styles mesh with me and how I complete my work? In this case I really did not even know the person or their style being they were just recently brought into the company. As I joined the call, there were already two people on the line. There was an introduction of someone from Human Resources (HR). My heart sunk; I knew what was about to happen. I have heard about this before, and heck, I was even a part of the conversations in the past. I did not expect that this meet and greet was going to be an HR call. I was completely blindsided. Immediately, I was in a state of shock. I listened carefully to my new "manager" talk about change and reorganizations, my department, and how my position was being eliminated. To be honest it was all a blur. I only heard some of the words. I tried to replay them in my head so I could understand them and what was coming next. At that point, my new "manager" said, "I will now hand it over to HR to explain your options". Then HR began to explain my options, rights, and next steps. I heard some of what was being said and was grateful when they said, "please take the rest of the day off to process this as it is a lot to take in."

I did just that; I signed off for the day. My head was swimming, and I was not sure what to think or do.

At this point I was in shock. I could not believe what happened because it all went down so fast. I did not know I was in shock at that point, and thoughts of denial swept over me. I was basically running things over in my head thinking, no, this could not be happening to me, I must have been mistaken. I am sure this is not the end of it, I think they will realize their mistake and ask me to stay. This must have been a mistake because I am a top performer. You guessed it; I was experiencing the first stage of the five stages of grief or loss: shock and denial. Looking back on it, I think it was more of a defense mechanism to give myself time to absorb the intensity of what just happened to me. In this stage you may also have feelings of being alone and isolated. I just kept saying to myself over and over, how could this happen? You are a top performer. Year after year your reviews were top of the company. Hi. My name is Frank DeMaio and I have been in the same place as you have. I have probably felt a lot of the same emotions you have been going through and I can tell you that it will get better. I am here to give you my perspective on job loss as it happened to me and also to provide you with some stories of other people who have been in the same situation as us.

When all this first happened to me, it was shocking, but looking back on it, it turned out to be a blessing in disguise. I had an inclination shortly after being given my notice that maybe this was a sign that I was supposed to move on and try new things and it turns out that was exactly what I needed. I found a position with a new company that gave me new challenges at work which I found to be extremely rewarding.

My experience in losing my job unexpectedly was a difficult time in my life. I remember what it felt like when I was separated from my position as well as all of the feelings that go along with it, like it was yesterday. I remember going through some of the stages of loss and the unnerving feelings and sometimes thinking "what am I going to do?"

This experience and the fearful feelings that I had steered me toward writing this book. It has helped me by allowing me to make sense of what happened, but the biggest purpose is to help others who are or have gone through the same thing but may not have experience, a network, or support system to help them through it. By providing a game plan and telling the stories about myself and others who have lost their job unexpectedly it can help those who are with working through a tough situation.

This book will also help guide you through the job search process and can help you make sense of the things you are going through by gaining the perspectives of others who have been in your shoes.

Throughout the job search process this book is going to teach you strategies such as:

- Suggestions on how to take care of your mental health after dealing with job loss.
- Helping you make career decisions to prepare for your future and continue to make forward progress.
- Strategies and tools for developing personal marketing materials to help you prepare for your job search.
- How to excel at the interviewing process.
- You're also going to hear stories of employees who have been in your shoes before, how they found opportunities in new organizations, and how these experiences turned out for the better for them.
- ...as well as many more ideas and tactics that you will find helpful.

Lastly, there are additional resources for you on losstoboss.com

You can email me at frank@losstoboss.com if you have any questions or need assistance. It may take me awhile to respond, but I will answer you.

While no one on their death bed has ever said, "I wish I spent more time at the office", the fact of the matter is, working is the way we provide for ourselves and our family. While you may be temporarily out of a position for now, stay positive and keep your confidence. If you have a job currently and are reading this book because you are looking to make a move, I say the same, stay positive and keep your confidence. There is something around the corner. Take this opportunity to put yourself on the right path. If you feel as though you aren't on the proverbial right path, this book can help you make a few small changes to get you where you need to be!

Chapter 2

Your Position Has Been Eliminated

Chances are if you are reading this book, you may have heard this during your career or quite possibly very recently, "I'm sorry, but your position has been eliminated." There are a couple of different scenarios that may have led you to this point.

Maybe you saw this coming due to a downturn of either the economy, the industry, your company, or your department. Unfortunately, this can happen in any position. When these occur companies sometimes call them many different things, such as furlough, layoffs, RIF (reduction in force), downsizing, reorganizations, restructuring, job elimination, etc.

Earlier in chapter one I talked about how *"My experience in losing my job unexpectedly was a difficult time in my life. I remember what it felt like when I was separated from my position as well as all of the feelings that go along with it, like it was yesterday. I remember going through some of the stages of loss and the unnerving feelings and sometimes thinking "what am I going to do?"*

The first of the five stages of loss hit me hard. Through the process, I checked most of the stages off the list. Each of them had their own mini process to move through and they include the following:

- ✓ Shock and Denial
- ✓ Anger
- ✓ Bargaining
- ✓ Depression
- ✓ Acceptance

After awhile, I started to get angry. I did not know who this new "boss" was, but I blamed him. I was angry at this person who I only met for all of five minutes. Yes, you guessed it, I was onto stage two: anger. I could not stop blaming and being angry. I wondered how this company could treat me like this after I gave them over a decade of my life. Didn't they realize all the great work I did for them every day? I continued to direct some of my anger at my "new" manager. However, this person was just brought into the company, this was not planned overnight, and it was part of a much larger reorganization, so chances are they probably were just told this is what was going to happen. Looking back on it, my anger was not really needed, and it was definitely misdirected, that is for sure. Part of this stage can also make you feel as though you were not valued for all that you did, and the sacrifices you made. This is all part of this stage.

After moving on from anger I began to run scenarios through my head. Why didn't I work more weekends? I should have volunteered for more projects outside of my regular work so they would have seen how much more valuable I was. If only I aligned myself within another department, I would not have been in the situation I was in. This was me being knee deep in the bargaining stage. In this stage you may also feel desperation which may lead you to appl to any and all jobs you see. This desperation may lead to a feeling of not being able to plan, not being able to network, and the potential of applying for jobs that you may be very overqualified, or underqualified for.

After I was shocked, angered, and began to bargain, I was lucky enough to move right to acceptance. I never went to the depression stage. In acceptance, my brain immediately began to realize that there is hope. I felt as though I could now do whatever I wanted to. I am not "stuck" in a job at this point, and I could move on to bigger and better things. I started to think of all the possibilities. Where would my life take me on my career path? I felt a sense of empowerment in being able to find something I enjoyed doing. I realized that I did not love what I was doing anyway. I had the opportunity to find something that would make me happy. Moving into the acceptance phase does not mean that what you experienced wasn't awful. It means that you are at the point where you realize that it happened, you cannot change it, but you can influence what happens next. I felt as though I could embrace it and find my next opportunity.

As I mentioned, I did not land on depression, but that does not mean it cannot happen or be a part of the process. You may have a sense of being overwhelmed. You may feel as though you cannot think, or you are confused. You can feel paralyzed. It can even feel as though you do not want to get off the couch or out of the bed. You may question your skills and value at this stage, which may lead you to stop looking for a job. Know that you are valuable. To get past this stage, it may be helpful to create a list of all the things you have done in the past which provided value to your employers. What are the contributions you have made?

On the next page, try filling out the simple chart in Figure 1. You can find a printable copy of this on my website www.losstoboss.com. This chart will help you to remember the contributions and value you bring to the table. Start by thinking about the positive contributions you made. What are the things that you have done while at work that you are proud of? Have you done a lot? Have you helped others and progressed the company? Have you increased profits for the company or possibly improved efficiencies? Have you helped customers? Write them down in the first column under positive contributions. After you brainstorm your list, begin to think about why each of those things are positive or valuable. Who or what did they benefit?

	Positive Contribution	Why it Was Valuable
1		
2		
3		
4		
5		

Figure 1.

Once you have this chart filled out, reflect on these contributions, and visualize the value you bring. Sometimes, we are so busy doing our thing that we forget to reflect and have self-realization of how valuable we are. This list will also help you later on when you are working on your resume. This can be a great pipeline of information to help you when writing your accomplishments and work tasks. Self-reflecting and focusing on your value are great tools to help you push through when you are feeling defeated. Remember that you are valuable!

Depression can be a landing place for loss. If you are unable to move past any of these stages, you should talk with a mental health expert. They can help with ways to cope with this loss. Staying in any one stage too long can be a detriment to your health and wellbeing.

You may or may not experience each of these five stages. The fact is, you will probably have some feelings of loss due to being unemployed. It is only natural to feel this way when your job is no longer there. Work can feel like a big part of a person's identity. Why do you think that is? When you are growing up you observe from an early age that work is important to your family's livelihood. You parents or caregivers probably did a lot of it. Plus, outside of sleep, work is probably the second biggest thing we do on a yearly basis. Yes, we have interests, hobbies, and personal relationships, but when you add up the time we spend on those specific things, work is still a bigger portion of your life. That is why we tend to identify ourselves with our work. An interesting thing here in the United States is that we tend to identify others with the work they do as well. How often do you meet someone and the first question that comes up is "So, what do you do for a living?"?

How much of our lives are taken up by work you ask? Well, let us do the math. There are 8,760 hours in a year. Typically, the average employee works 40 hours per week with 2 weeks off for vacation. That equates to us working approximately 2000 hours per year. That means without overtime, commuting, or any potential extra hours (weekends etc.), we work approximately 23% of our lives in any given year. One very staggering number when you think about it, is if we start working when we are 25, and many of us start much earlier, and work until we are 65, with many of us working well past that, we will work approximately 80,000 hours in our lifetime. Wow, that really adds up, so it is only natural for one to align themselves with their work and feel a loss when it is not there anymore.

You can get past these stages of loss by knowing your value and focusing on what's next. Take this opportunity to realize you are not your work. You should work to live and not live to work. Getting this opportunity to step back and have this realization, can help you to have a new perspective on life. With a working to live mindset you can reinvent what makes you happy and motivates you.

Acknowledge the pain you have and accept that the loss can trigger many strange and unexpected emotions. The process will be unique to you but find support from people who care about you. Be sure to continuously practice self-care so you can support yourself emotionally.

Sometimes when you work in certain industries this can happen more often. Take Joe for example. Joe was a latecomer to fatherhood and married at 42 leading him to raising young children while in his late 40s. Joe has held numerous positions in a sales hunter role. Each time he was separated from his jobs, he was forced to pick himself up and continue. Here is a brief outline of the times he had to work through transitions from one job to another.

Joe's journey in a sales hunter role began when he was hired into a sales role at a globally known copier/printer company as an Account Executive. He worked there for three years which were full of success and many accolades. Joe was recruited by a competitor copier company as an Account Executive and decided to leave the company. It came as a complete surprise when he was fired from the position. When it happened, he was so frustrated, mad, surprised, and embarrassed that he didn't tell family or friends for two weeks. He could only bring himself to tell a couple of very close mentors.

He went on to work for a medical device company as a Territory Sales Manager. He was on a 30-day performance improvement plan (PIP) when he received a surprise call informing him that he was fired. Even though he was on this 30-day plan, it still came as a shock when he was told. He felt annoyed and angry at first, but came to accept it after a few days.

He had tried extremely hard to bring up the numbers while in this position. There were a couple of different factors that were too challenging to overcome in the time frame the company gave him. The first challenge was that it was a brand-new territory for this 'neurological' division and the patient population who needed devices in this region were low. The reason why being fired was such a surprise is that even with these challenges he was able to work his way up to 80% of the target.

Joe went on to an enterprise software development company as an

Inside Sales Account Executive. He spent two and a half years working inside sales and he really loved this job. He had a lot of success and even made the President's Club (high award for top sales). He sought out and won a promotion to Field Account Executive. During his first six months in the position, his direct manager changed three times. The last manager he was given had very limited experience and because of some personality differences he and Joe didn't see eye to eye. He finished up the fiscal year strong with the closing of a large $1.3M deal. He finished at 135% of his quota and was extremely happy. Joe landed this deal by working side by side with upper management to create a good cop bad cop routine. Unfortunately, on the very last day of the fiscal year his manager fired him. He was completely caught off guard and initially he was terribly upset, embarrassed, and distraught. The good part was that he didn't have to deal with a bad manager anymore and was still able to collect an exceptionally large commission check.

Shortly afterwards he was recruited to a small regional software value added reseller (VAR) as a Territory Account Executive. He spent two and a half years there and had some amazing success. He won President's Club and exceeded his quota for 80% of the time he was employed there. In his final three months, he started losing respect for the decisions of the company owners. On top of that he was also getting a bit burned out on the prospecting activity. The company went from 25 employees to 6 employees fairly rapidly due to some interpersonal and legal issues. He was ultimately relieved when he was fired unexpectedly. There were a lot of stressors with the job, and it came as a blessing.

His next position was a Territory Account Executive with a regional network and software integrator company. Overall revenue numbers weren't working out and he was fired unexpectedly.

He took on a Territory Sales Manager role at a very small software value added reseller (VAR) shortly after. He worked hard but felt great about what he was able to accomplish. He was proud of how he carried himself with integrity and honesty. Unfortunately, him and his manager's personality didn't mesh well. On top of that, his manager was an insatiable micro manager. It was so bad that he gave his manager a nickname that he would use lightly and only with his wife, "Jekyll and Hyde". This personality conflict ultimately led to Joe being fired.

Joe then moved on to an Account Executive at a large enterprise software provider when he was recruited by former colleagues. He was again unexpectedly fired. Joe read the writing on the wall. There were some significant changes with the corporate environment that lead to territory changes. These changes had a huge impact on his pipeline which left him very little to work with.

Some may look at these transitions and think, "why would anyone want to be in such a volatile industry that leads to so many stops and starts?"

Joe has made a conscious decision not to go into pure marketing roles, full time project management, or into a role where he is managing other people. He knows he has the skills to do this type of work, but it's not what he enjoys. Staring at a blank screen trying to come up with a few brilliant marketing lines to inspire curiosity about a product is one of his least favorite professional tasks.

He prefers the idea of staying in his sales hunter role where he gets to interface with highly intelligent, qualified, and talented people. He has a deep, fundamental, belief that there lies, in each of us, a strong natural role fit: weaving together a set of strengths that align to an ideal job that is the absolute best job for each of us. A job that will both stretch our skills to grow as individuals and put our true personal strengths to work.

Sales representatives (common titles of Account Executive, Account Manager, Regional Sales Director, Territory Account Manager, Inside Sales Representative, VP Sales, etc.) have a classic persona of being outgoing, driven, goal oriented, well spoken, type-A personalities. Joe feels as though he aligns to these traits. He has about 80% of these in the bag and still works on the other 20%. We all play the game of comparing ourselves to our colleagues, but he stands on his own when it comes to the value he brings to the table.

There is an art and science to a sales process and to the individual approach each salesperson takes to prospect, present, and close on deals.

In his sixteen years of carrying a quota Joe can easily say he is not the absolute best, most amazing salesperson. He is a very hard-working professional salesperson who genuinely enjoys the industry and products he's sold. For many years he was in the top 10% of the salesforce at the companies he worked for. He followed the guidance of hundreds of hours of sales training and has read a litany of over 100 books on sales and sales methodologies. Joe has some natural gifts in the areas of pipeline development: the thick skin needed to deal with objections, rejections, and the pure difficulty of prospecting with only a phone and list of phone numbers. He is naturally capable of presenting in front of groups, learning, delivering a message to select groups of prospective buyers, and managing complex sales cycles with hundreds of diverse buyers involved. He can cold call with the best. He had a three year stretch where he was making around 50 cold calls per day across two different jobs.

There may be some who read this thinking about how they've faced the same challenges in a sales career. There could be some of you who are thinking about going into a sales career who read all of these details and think, 'Hey I can not only handle that, but I know I have the talent, skills, creativity, thick skin and determination to succeed anyway'. Some of you may be thinking, "This isn't for me, but I know I'd be great in supporting front-line sales in another say such as product development, engineering, design, etc."

Joe believes there are two reasons as to why his career was set in motion toward the path of sales. One of his first memories of him being in sales was in grade school when he was named a 'super salesperson'. He won first place in 6th through 8th grade fund-raising where he sold the most chocolate bars. His second came from a loving warning from his dad, with whom he has a great

Relationship. His says his father has a wonderful personality, is an outgoing story and joke teller, and a smart civil engineer. When his father was in his first few years of professional work with a large American multinational corporation he was encouraged to go into sales. After many conversations he learned that salespeople could have amazing careers but tend to go through 'good and bad years' with their salaries and commissions. His father knew at that young age he wanted to become a father and raise children. His gut feeling told him that going towards a more stable salary would be a better foundation for family life. He told this to Joe in his early days of talking about interviewing in sales. Those words stayed in Joe's thoughts for years. Every time he thought about those words of wisdom, he brushed them off because he thought 'well I think I have that knack for doing sales'.

Joe feels as though he's come a long way in sixteen years of corporate technology sales jobs. As he moves into parenting little kids, he no longer wants the added stresses of 'good and bad years'. A stable salary is looking better and better to him at this point.

His most recent layoff was respectfully called 'involuntary layoff due to performance on revenue expectations'. The separation was specifically for an Account Executive role. He was told he was welcome to apply for other roles in the company and was provided with eligibility for unemployment benefits.

What he's come to learn is that these roles may be just right for some people at a certain time of life, or for a certain kind of personality. We put forward different aspects of our personalities in order to take on different roles at different times of life. This doesn't mean we are giving up (on said challenges) or changing our personality. There is also some truth to the fact that different market conditions in different geographical territories will set some people up for huge success and in other geographical territories, not so much. Joe says it's also worth pointing out that different aspects of roles become of higher importance to us as different times. It

could be our desire for financial stability or for the goals we have set for ourselves. At this point in his career with two little children, a young family who is open to having more kids, he wants to move toward roles that tend to be long lasting. He wants to move away from roles presenting higher risks of firing. He wants to avoid the periodic layoffs. There are stresses associated to being fired and having to hunt for new jobs on a regular basis. The emotions of Joe's experience with job loss and being fired have gone on a journey of their own. His response to his first lay-off experience thirteen years ago was more of shame and embarrassment. He took a full week or two of personal alone time dealing with his mental process of coming to accept the layoff. He was glad that he wasn't yet a father with a mortgage and that he wasn't living above his means. He's not sure how he would have responded but the emotional rollercoaster could have been a lot worse. Even though firing managers were firm but gentle in their delivery of letting him go it also made him wonder if he was meant to stay in sales. For a long time after, these thoughts stuck around for him to internalize. The comments made him struggle at times with his self-belief in doing certain aspects of these roles. He had feelings of shock, denial, and anger but he was able to move past them- sometimes quicker such as during a period of time in mid-2009 when there were a ton of other layoffs happening. Each time he was laid off, these emotions would come back again.

In his most recent layoff, he caught up with a handful of fellow salespeople who have held long careers in these roles. He was processing the experience with them and discussing companies and roles to go hunt for. He learned there are tons of salespeople who develop such a thick skin and almost bull headedness about experiencing layoffs. During those conversations one 30-year veteran had 15 jobs over that time frame, some of which include founding companies, VP sales, Account Executive and Global Sales Director. This experienced sales veteran said 'he no longer cares' about the periodic layoffs he has experienced. He had reached a

point in his late 40s and early 50s where his kids were grown and out of college when he came to terms with it. The many successes that he had over his career are what started to really stand out to him. The failures were blended into a distant memory in the rearview mirror of his life. While on one hand that is a great place to find yourself, the road getting there is not necessarily a path many will take. The path can have many big ups and downs. It takes strength to weather the storm.

You must be confident in knowing that you have the skills necessary, as well as the desire, patience, obedience, and sense of focus to do a role. For anyone wanting to become an Account Executive (or any role with a high expectation of revenue generation through growing new sales opportunities, business development and closing new logo accounts) you must be willing to go through either an annual or nearly annual change in business expectations. These expectations around territory, product marketing, manager changes, and account dynamic changes, will impact the pipeline you've been working on. It may also incur an annual or nearly annual job-loss or job-change. These losses and changes will require a healthy amount of networking, job-seeking, and interviewing. If you have a high emotional IQ and are a rare sales champion, you are in the right role. These champions always seem to be ahead of the changes coming with internal politics and manage to get recruited with better offers at other companies.

Joe is good in the role of target account development, sending out marketing emails, and making necessary cold and warm calls to develop new business relationships. While he might be good at it, he doesn't love it, and not many people really do. He knows he has a passion for working with customers to help them get the most out of the products he sells. He enjoys helping them through challenging times. This is his career sweet spot and aligns to his new role as a Customer Success Manager. He wonders if this is the role he should have moved to sooner.

More than a few times in Joe's career he decided to take a certification course, above what was expected, in order to help him excel in the day-to-day role. Many times, he completed these certifications on evenings and weekends. This self-imposed training has ranged from technical skills, platform expertise, interpersonal skills, selling, or negotiation skills.

He has achieved a Project Management Institute (PMI) and Project Management Professional (PMP) certificate which he highly recommends for anyone who believes they may be cut out to be a Project Manager.

Joe says Toastmasters has also been an invaluable resource for him. He spent about 3 years working through their first 2 levels of certification which is Competent Communication and Competent Leadership. He says it's an excellent way to practice public speaking, improve your sphere of influence, and build your leadership ability. The cost of Toastmasters is very minimal compared to the value and training you receive.

In one of his positions, he was lucky enough to have been referred into a one-year Leadership Development Program (LDP) which was an incredible experience.

Careers can take some unexpected turns and can throw you curveballs, but it's about knowing what you are good at, what you want, and keeping to your path.

Hearing about Joe's experience shows how sometimes you can see it coming, but even worse, you can also sometimes be taken completely off guard.

You may be in a situation where you are not sure what happened. Maybe you thought you were doing all the right things, or possibly even highly successful things for the company, but this situation just snuck up on you.

Sometimes it has nothing to do with you. It is just part of the larger vision or re-organization where your position doesn't exist anymore.

Other times it is more about you directly. Great employees are fired by companies all the time. There are many reasons for this. Working for poor leadership can lead to issues you may not realize. Some common reasons why great employees get fired are listed below. Be sure when you read them you understand that just because they are listed does not mean you should stop doing them. There are only two reasons they are listed: poor leadership and poor company values. Being let go from a company for any of these reasons shows that not every company deserves your skills. It is their loss and not yours.

1. You had a better idea or have better ideas than your boss.
2. You tried to set normal work life balance boundaries by saying I will pick this back up on Monday instead of taking it home and working on it over the weekend.
3. You asked questions no one wanted to face because they were too difficult to tackle.
4. Your immediate boss did not like all the attention you were getting for a job well done by upper management and felt threatened.
5. It looked like you were making others look bad by doing so well and achieving so much.
6. Your boss thought you were so good you were going to take their job next.

Whatever the reason is that you are no longer employed is not really the subject of this book. We are not here to talk about the legalities of you being let go or if you have legal recourse or not. You will have to consult a lawyer for that. I am not here to talk about a company's poor work culture, bosses, non-leaders, etc. I am just going to say, it's great that you no longer have to deal with any of that now. You'll have to consult other resources if you want to learn more about severance packages, or unemployment processes.

This is about what to do now that you are in the situation you are in, what steps you can take to process this and come out on the other end better than you were. The unfortunate fact of the matter is that being fired happens to great employees all the time and there is nothing dishonorable about it. Lucky for you there are a lot of resources out there to help you move on to the next chapter of your life, and this book can be one of those resources.

Chapter 3

Changes For The Better

You have probably been so dedicated to the place you have worked that you may have let other things slide. Typically, things related directly to yourself have taken a back burner. You have probably not paid as close attention to yourself as you should have, because so much of your time was taken up with working.

You may have been like Brian. His company forced him to do more with less, which led to being overworked. He was working day and night.

Brian worked for a financial institution in the IT department. His team focused on building, securing, and maintaining various servers which also included 24/7 support. In addition to his normal team responsibilities, he was also accountable for ensuring all the company's servers received their security updates and validated they were successful.

During a reorganization of his department, his team was reduced from eleven to five. He was one of the team members who remained after the reduction in force. Of course, with the reduction, it increased his team's per person workload immensely. The work remained the same but the number of people available to help with tasks was cut by more than half.

After a few months, one of the engineers left for another opportunity. This reduced the team yet again. The team of four was told that the position would be filled, and they would also get some relief with their overnight tasks from an offshore team. Unfortunately, after a year, that engineer position was never backfilled and sadly their production suffered. For Brian and the team what suffered the most was the nonexistent work/life balance. Looking back, he realized that even though he felt very overworked, he liked what he was doing. He felt as though the work was making a positive impact on the organization. There was a sense of pride knowing they were able to accomplish so much with such a small team. He often thought about what they might have been able to accomplish if his company had even hired just two more experienced engineers.

One week prior to Thanksgiving 2019, Brian and his team were informed that they were being outsourced.

He recalls that it did not hit him at first. In fact, he suddenly had time that he never had before. It was a great holiday season for him and his family. He was not on call and did not have to perform any of his off-hours tasks. The holidays were excellent and went by quickly. Once January hit though, he started to realize how devastated he was. He felt as though he worked so hard to get into that role. Now he would wake up in the morning looking for work related problems to solve only to be left with an emptiness inside himself because there were none.

Looking back, he realizes that he was in shock at first. He experienced a feeling of surrealness when he woke up each morning. He did not have any ticket queues or reports to review, or meetings to attend. After living that life for so long it was tough to be without it. He said he never became angry, but he did feel as though he was getting a little depressed. The timing of his team being outsourced was just a few months prior to the 2020 pandemic. The pandemic changed the job market considerably. The issues he had to deal with were compounded by mass unemployment, national civil unrest and some family health concerns. He said the year was like a perfect storm in many ways for him and his family.

Throughout it all, he never let himself get too down. He kept himself busy and tried to have as much fun as possible while being in a pandemic lockdown.

He was able to walk his kids to and from school every day during the spring, spend more time with his mother, reconnect with distant family, old friends, and past colleagues. These were things he had not had time for in quite awhile. He even tackled some of the projects around the house that had taken a back burner.

He realistically understood that the change had happened, but he said he never really got to the acceptance stage emotionally until the summer of 2020. His acceptance stemmed from a couple of different places. One was being able to process the fact that he wasn't actually fired.

When he was separated from his company, he was told that he was not being fired, but that it was due to his role not existing anymore. They told him that if another position were to ever come up that he was a fit for he would be welcomed back after going through the normal application process. There was something about hearing that from Human Resources and his Managers that helped him.

"I've always believed in myself. I think what helped most was my confidence and knowing that my work was appreciated, and they would hire me again was a boost."

The second area of acceptance came from his ability to use his newfound time to spend it with his family. It felt good to him to be able to make up for missing the past couple of summers due to work. He and his family hiked, cooked together, and played and invented new games. They also engaged in many activities including socially distanced disc golf.

He drew strength from his family. Knowing he was responsible for them is what kept him going.

During this time, he took advantage of some of the outplacement services his company provided him with. Brian took some courses with LinkedIn Learning and Code Academy to improve and sharpen his skills.

"I think what really helped the most was just having a routine and some discipline. By mid-summer, reinventing myself and finding my next job became my full-time job."

He filled his days with courses, job fairs, recruiter meetings, and lab projects of his own. This included rebuilding his own lab server to practice and keep up on his skills.

Even though it was not quite clear at the beginning, Brian can now see that he was given a rare opportunity. Due to a generous severance package, he had a little runway to re-invent and redirect his career. Being out of work during that time was a blessing in disguise. He was able to put all his energy into his family which is invaluable. He had made a bad habit out of prioritizing work over family, and this gave him an opportunity to reverse that.

It took Brian about one year, but he was able to obtain a position in a large tech company. The position and company come with a bright future with many opportunities for growth.

It came about through being confident, staying patient and remaining focused. He attributes networking as being extremely valuable to him because a recommendation for the new opportunity came to him from his network. Networking with others gave him confidence, while job transition courses helped him to prepare and gave him some industry perspective.

He is in a much better place in his new job role than he was prior to the separation. He still misses working with people from his old job and many aspects of being there, but his new company offers him a culture that is more in alignment with his own. He has balance, better benefits, and great technology to work on. His new company emphasizes community and work/life balance which he was missing before.

Brian's tip for those who have lost their job, or for those who are job hunting, is to learn about best practices around ATS compliance. He also recommends having a professional resume review if possible.

Looking back, he realizes the change started to feel right. Losing his job was a gift disguised as a failure. It just took him time to see it correctly. While the experience feels oddly invaluable, he would rather not go through it again.

His advice is to not lose confidence, keep perspective, and do not look back. Change is necessary even when it is not exactly planned. Embrace the opportunity and push forward.

If you can relate to Brian, this could be a time to improve yourself in different areas. You must decide for yourself what areas have been shelved and need to be taken down, dusted off, and used. Here are some suggested areas to look at.

You can focus on your health by engaging in more exercise or take the time to eat healthier. Maybe take up a new sport that you've been wanting to try or that new hobby. It's quite possible you could incorporate some daily meditation or breathing exercises into your daily routine. There are a lot of resources online that can help you get started if you have never done that before. Maybe start your day with a gratitude practice. While you may have lost your job, there are a lot of other things in your life to be grateful for. Make a list of those things and read it every day. Focusing on the positives in life is a game changer.

Reading either for pleasure or learning is another area that could be brought back into the fold. There are many benefits to reading: as it can: produce improvement in brain activity, lower blood pressure and heart rate, fight depression symptoms, help prevent cognitive reduction, help to prepare you for sleep, increase your vocabulary and comprehension, and help you learn about different perspectives while improving your knowledge, just to name a few.

Take this time to reduce bad habits and create new positive ones. You are onto a new adventure and now is the time to prepare yourself with a new outlook.

You can also look for other outlets for your knowledge and expertise. Maybe start a blog, or a Facebook group to network and share information. Meet with friends and key contacts for networking opportunities. Think about consulting with small businesses and volunteer organizations, publish an article, or a newsletter. Volunteering at a nonprofit can also help you to grow as a person. Look to stretch your limits and try new things.

This is also a great time to invest in yourself. Any time is a great time to invest in yourself but sometimes we do not always have the hours to be able to do that. Look for education and trainings that you are interested in and that can help up you to "level-up". There are a lot of things like this for free on the internet. How to videos can teach you quite a bit. Taking ownership for your skills and abilities can open many doors for you. It is possible you may want to hire a coach, takes some classes, enroll in higher learning, or attend conferences and events. Any money spent for self-improvement is a long-term investment that no one can ever take away from you. Investing in yourself can help put you in the mindset to realize that you are worth it and that you matter.

In addition to thinking about how you can "level up" you should begin to formally map out your path. Brainstorm and write out the goals you have for yourself. You may not have had time to do this previously, but it can be a great benefit to you and your mind to write out your 30, 60, or 90-day goals. You can utilize a simple template such as in Figure 2 on the next page to help you with organizing your goals. You can find a free template like this on my website at www.losstoboss.com to use. Being able to see your goals on paper can help your mind to start formulating how you will achieve them. Once you have a 90-day plan, look to stretch it out to define six month, one year, and five-year goals as well.

"Do something today that your future self will thank you for." –Sean Patrick Flanery [1]

	Category	Description	Tasks
30 Day Goals			
1			
2			
3			
4			
5			
60 Day Goals			
1			
2			
3			
4			
5			
90 Day Goals			
1			
2			
3			
4			
5			
6 Month Goals			
1			
2			
3			
4			
5			
1 Year Goals			
1			
2			
3			
4			
5			
5 Year Goals			
1			
2			
3			
4			
5			
10 Year Goals			
1			
2			
3			
4			
5			

Figure 2.

There are many things that can be done to make progress when you are unemployed and looking for employment. You must take ownership for your own career path and put in the work to find work.

In fact, when I coach people who are currently employed, I always tell them that they must take responsibility for their own career. They cannot rely on managers, leaders, CEOs, etc. to drive their career, they must do that themselves. They should have a career plan outlined that shows their long-term goals with short term tasks that get them to those goals. It is the same for someone who is out of work. It is a terrible feeling to look back on one, two, or five years and say, "I have not really done a lot to progress my career. I am pretty much in the same boat as I was in when I started this." It is extremely easy to get so bogged down in your day-to-day work that you forget about self-care. You must invest in yourself to achieve what you want to achieve. If you do not already, make it a point to not let another day go by where you are not owning your path. Make a change for the better and remember you've got this!

Chapter 4

Persevere, Endure, Succeed

"Our greatest glory is not in never falling, but in rising every time we fall." – Confucius [2]

If you are looking to rebound from job loss know that you can and will get through this. If you are looking to make a career change, it is not impossible. There are others who have walked this same exact path with tremendous success.

You are a powerful person who can do whatever you set your mind to. Focus on your strengths which will help drive you toward the successes you have in mind for yourself.

"Your mind is powerful. When you fill it with positive thoughts your life will start to change." – Buddha [3]

Sometimes understanding that other people have been through the same hard knocks as you and have come out on the other side better than before can boost your morale and help you to realize you can handle more than you originally thought. It can give you a sense of confidence in overcoming the challenges set before you.

Hearing about real world examples and people who have been through the grind can give you a perspective you never had before. Gaining insight from someone who has firsthand knowledge of what you are going through can lead you toward success. Why reinvent the wheel when you can learn from those before you?

Take Mike, for example. When he felt like the world gave him a punch in the face, he picked himself up and carried on.

Mike started his career as a CPA in the private industry and moved from a divisional controller to a corporate controller and VP of Finance and CFO by the age of 29.

His longest tenured position was in the printing industry, for a book manufacturer. They printed and bound novels, textbooks, bibles, and reference books.

He was responsible for all aspects of the company's financial operations including accounting, cash management, banking relations, human resources, information systems and technology. Eventually he also assumed the role of chief operating officer including sales management, union relations and operations.

In 2010, the owner had agreed to sell the company to him with the stipulation that he had two months to secure financing. While he was able to secure the financing, there were delays, and out of nowhere the company was sold to a former employee for more money.

Mike was not told about the counteroffer or the sale to the other party until the day of the sale. The owner told him privately that he was announcing the sale of the company, to the entire work force and that Mike would need to make his own arrangements with the new owners. The acquiring company already had a CFO, and he did not wish to work for the new organization. The easy part for him was knowing that he did not care for the new owners and wanted nothing to do with the business. He did not like the type of business they practiced or the kind of people they were. Acceptance is knowing that he did everything possible to reach his goal and it did not happen- no regrets and no time to spend looking back.

What had transpired did not surprise him in the least, but what did, was the fact that they only offered three month's severance after 24 years of service. By comparison, a company recently gave him two months of severance after one year of service on an interim position. He was always told he would be taken care of if there was a sale, but

that did not happen. With two children in college and one in law school he had to go home and tell his wife that he had placed his trust in the wrong person.

Due to the sale of the company, it was difficult for him to be positive about the future with all the employees that had come to trust him. He felt sad, frustrated, and disappointed that all the hard work and goals accomplished were wasted. On top of that he felt a sense of a personal relationship loss as the owner would invite him and his wife to Christmas parties and other gatherings. Looking back, he now realizes the owner had changed by becoming bitter, forgetful, and paranoid.

Three years after the sale, the new organization was forced to file bankruptcy. The same company that had made a profit in 23 of the 24 years Mike was employed there was liquidated.

Mike says he felt isolation and guilt for not spending more time building a peer network. To his surprise the quality of work he had done over the years had been building a network. Many business associates offered to help and within two months he accepted an offer in another state with a commercial printing company. The position was of equal compensation, but it required him to live out of state during the week and return home on the weekends.

He said that even after all this time, he still feels anger, but he does not let it consume him and he tries to be the more evolved human. For years he refused to have any prospective employers contact the owner about his job performance while with his previous company even though all the headhunters told him it would be viewed as a negative. He just felt as if he did not want to give the owner another chance to stab him in the back. Interestingly, when he left a company in 2019, 7 years later, one of the companies he interviewed with called the owner for a reference without his approval. It turns out he knew the owner and offered him the position based on, in part, an incredibly positive recommendation.

Desperation for him was allowing himself to be dragged to every business event in his home area, to network, by his father-in-law, who Mike says is a wonderful man. His father-in-law did not want

him to find a position far away which would require him to move his family away. He was able to find a compromise with traveling back and forth during the week and on weekends. This was all because of the network he had built through his work ethic and capability and without even realizing it.

> **"Staying positive is extremely difficult when everyone is doubting your value and abilities."**

Mike credits his participation in high school sports for the internal grit to continue, and for instilling the belief that you have value as a person and as a contributing member of society. He has remained on the path of play hard, work hard, and never ever give up.

> **"Acceptance comes with time in situations like this."**

For Mike, the worst part of losing a job was not knowing how to provide for his family.

The business network that was built without him realizing was made up of his father-in-law, his wife, children, and him and his wife's brother and sisters. They knew how dedicated and how hard he had worked and they all felt a sense of anger on his behalf. One of his contacts suggested he join Financial Executive Network Group (FENG). Although he has not landed a position through them, their daily newsletter, leads, and positive realistic advice has been great.

He thought one of the first things he would do after being unemployed would be to go to a movie in the middle of the afternoon, but he never did. Looking back, he says looking for a new position that pays enough and leaves some dignity is a full-time job. He did renew his CPA license, which was frustrating, but did make him more marketable. He also worked on his Excel and

technology skills.

Looking back, the biggest benefit to losing his job was, proving to himself and subsequent companies that he does have the

knowledge, skill, and temperament to excel in other situations. His experience has made him take life less seriously these days. His wife gave him an Apple watch, but he stopped wearing it. He has not set the alarm clock in four years. He goes to bed a little earlier these days and sees his general physician for annual checkups. He has more time to reach out to his brother and sister. He even grew a beard for the first time in his life.

"I always felt I had to carry the company, now I just help to carry the company."

After five years travelling out of state during the week for work, he found a position closer to home where he has been for two years as CFO.

He says he is much better off with the new company which allows him the freedom, resources, and time to make a difference.

His advice is to work hard, work smart, assess, and plan. He leveraged Zip, Indeed, industry network, his business network, and his personal network in his job searches. He recommends interviewing for the "not perfect" jobs as some are surprises and some can become referrals. Sometimes taking a lower paying job with growth potential is an opportunity.

When people ask about the sale of the book manufacturer and what happened to him, he says that it was a wonderful opportunity to show, not tell, his children what you do when life is not fair, and it gives you a kick. To show them when bad things happen you are not a victim, and you are not defined by the bad thing. The bad thing just happened, and you move forward, stay positive and work hard.

Chapter 5

Self Reflection, Evaluation, and Taking Stock

Before we begin this chapter, let's quickly recap what we've covered so far and what you've accomplished. You've read advice on how to be aware of your mental health, so that you're ready to prepare and excel in the next stages in your career. You've filled out your chart of positive contributions and values that you bring to the table. You've brainstormed and written out future goals for yourself using the worksheet. You've read success stories of other colleagues who have been in similar scenarios involving their careers, and in turn how they overcame adversity to blast through their plateaus and take their careers to the next level. This chapter is when we begin to prepare for putting together an action plan of steps for you to break through your own plateaus to take your career to the next level!

Step 1 – Taking Inventory

You may be thinking what am I going to do next? What should I be pursuing or doing at this point? This chapter is about self-reflection, evaluation, and taking stock of what you have in your personal inventory. Trust me, you have a great inventory; you just need to take stock to understand what it is.

Taking inventory, is about identifying your interests, skills, personality, values, work experience, educational background, professional certifications, and everything else that makes up you. This is also a time for self-reflecting on what your personal restrictions may be. What is holding you back from taking yourself

to the next level? Being able to outline what those personal restrictions might be is the first step in formulating a plan to overcome them. Getting past personal restrictions will give you a boost of success.

Working your way through the process of self-inventorying your strengths and restrictions will get you poised for victory. It will enable you to succeed in your job search and career planning. These exercises will take the accident out of landing a job or the need for trial and error. Yes, there are times when you might just accidently, or by some strange stroke of luck, land your dream job. That does not happen very often, but if you are looking for your dream job, you can increase your chances of making that happen by doing research and self-exploration to set you off on the correct path.

The unfortunate fact of the matter is we are often pigeonholed into a career that is paying the right amount of money, is for convenience, or possibly because someone else thinks that would be a good job for us. Someone else may think that the job would be right for you because it is renowned and they would be proud of you if you had that job, or they think that is the type of job you would be good at. If you choose a job because of someone else, it is inevitable that you are not going to love it down the road. It can't be someone else that wants it for you. You have to want it for yourself.

It is like quitting a bad habit. Your friend or partner could tell you repeatedly you need to quit biting your nails, or smoking, or whatever it may be, but ultimately you are not going to be happy doing it until you decide that quitting is what you want to do. The fact of the matter is that the ideal scenario is that we need it to be in alignment with who we are, and that will lead you to prosper.

"You can only become truly accomplished at something you love. Don't make money your goal. Instead pursue the things you love doing and then do them so well that people can't take their eyes off of you." - Maya Angelou [4]

By looking at your skills and interests and becoming self-aware you should be able to find an area that will align to a job you will excel at.

One of the best ways to evaluate your skills, interests, and personality is to take an assessment or two. By assessment I do not mean a test with right and wrong answers. With an assessment there are no right and wrong answers, just answers that are yours. The assessments I am referring to do not measure intellect. They are to explore yourself to find career options that align with your skills and interests.

The assessment examples I have listed each have different purposes and value which can help you to gain valuable insight into yourself. You may have heard of some of these or you may have already taken some of them, which is great. Utilize those assessments that you have taken in the past to help you with your plan. If you have not taken any of these before I recommend you take at least one.

I do not recommend any specific one of these assessments on this list for you as it is hard for me to understand your specific situation. You will have to research them yourself to determine which one might be right for you. If you cannot decide which one to take do not stop there. Pick one and move forward. In life it is better to act, and course correct later on, than to take no action at all. In fact, keep in mind that there is power in making decisions quickly and changing your mind slowly.

I have taken some of these and found them to be especially useful. I have taken the Myers Briggs Type Indicator as well as the Strengths Finder 2.0. Strengths Finder 2.0 can help you discover the things you do best and help you to turn your talents into strengths. I have taken this assessment a couple of times now and have had people I have coached take it as well. It is interesting to gain some inner perspective on your talents which can help guide you toward jobs of interest.

Assessment Examples:

- o Myers Briggs Type Indicator (MBTI)
- o Keirsey Temperament Sorter
- o True Colors
- o DISC Assessment
- o HEXACO Personality Inventory
- o Holland Code Career Test
- o MAPP Test
- o iSeek "Clusters"
- o MyPlan
- o Strengths Finder 2.0

The list provides you with some areas to research further. It will help you to determine what each assessment is about, and if it is beneficial for you to take them. These may help you find something out about yourself you did not know, or can even be a validation of things you already know. Get exploring!

<u>Step 2 - Brainstorming</u>

You have given yourself an assessment and have worked toward your inventory which is a great start. You will now start to explore the feelings you have about certain work areas.

Take out a piece of paper or a white board and write in the middle, "What do I want to be when I grow up?". Next draw a line off to the side and write something down that answers that. Continue brainstorming ideas over and over until you run out. Keep in mind when brainstorming that there are no rules, there are no limits. Feasibility is not important at this step and should not be taken into consideration. Do not shoot down any ideas that pop into your head, write them down. Focusing on the quality of the idea is not allowed. Whatever pops into your head is written down, record everything!

"It takes courage to grow up and become who you really are." - E.E. Cummings [5]

Figure 3 on the next page is an example of what this looks like. You can also download this template for free on www.losstoboss.com.

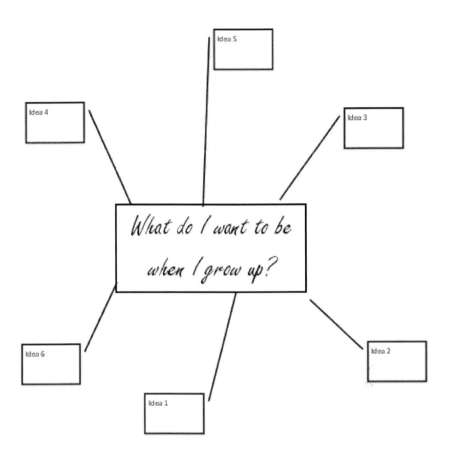

Figure 3.

After you complete the "What do I want to be when I grow up?" exercise, you should look to answer some additional questions as well. This is a list of examples that you can use during these brainstorming sessions. Do not be afraid to come up with your own questions. If you have something you want to find an answer to, this can help you.

- What type of employment would best utilize my skills and interests?
- What type of work environment am I attracted to?
- What role do I want to play within an organization?
- How does my management style mesh with my career objective?
- How will this career impact other areas of my life?
- Does this fit with my values?
- What are the top five things that are important to me for job satisfaction?

Once you have completed your brainstorming sessions, explore offshoots of what you wrote by drawing lines around those boxes and coming up with more ideas relative to each one of those. This will help you to begin formulating your thoughts and ideas.

These diagrams can now be used to point to your top choices. Look at them and circle the ones that are your best options and make the most sense to you. Next, you will want to begin narrowing your list down as there might be ones that just won't work for you. Draw a line through those and focus on the ones that do. Once you have your list write them down on a separate piece of paper.

Step 3 – Aligning Your Research and Making Career Decisions

You have done some self-exploration up until this point, and now it is about beginning to put the puzzle pieces together. Alignment is about determining what job, career, or work aligns to your skills, interests, personality, and brainstorms.

Now that you have your assessments complete, review the information you received. Analyze it to determine what may and may not feel right to you. That information should then be evaluated alongside your brainstorming session to identify areas that might be right for you. Things that align to your skills, interests, and personality are where you want to explore more. Armed with this information, your next step will be to research occupations that have similar alignment to your self-reflection and evaluation.

You may be asking "how do I do that? Where do I go to understand what possibilities are out there?" You will need to research various career fields to find options that would be good for you. Without this, you will be limited in being able to make a choice that benefits you. A great resource for this investigation is a website put out by the United States Department of Labor which can be found here: https://www.mynextmove.org/.

There are a couple of different ways you can utilize this resource. The first being, you can type in some keywords based on our interests. For example, if you said you were interested in becoming a firefighter, you can type "firefighter" in and once you search it will present you with a list of occupations related to firefighter. That list is important as it can present ideas that you never even thought of in that occupational space. If you find an occupation you think sounds interesting, you can delve deeper into it with another click.

It will tell you some excellent information that will help you to determine if it aligns to your skills, interests, and personality.

Here are some examples of the topics the search covers. Again, this list uses the firefighter example from above.

- What does a firefighter do?
- What would a firefighter do on the job?
- What are some of the knowledge, skills, and abilities you might need to be a firefighter?
- What type of personality traits are helpful to be a firefighter?
- What technology you may need to work with?
- Education recommendations
- Salary minimum, maximum, and average
- Job outlook (will the job be in demand in the future?)
- There is even a list of links for further investigation

This becomes a fun game at this point as you have a lot of key job information at your fingertips. Your mission at this point is to research as many job interests as possible that are from your brainstorming session. You are going to want to explore and dive as deep as you can to evaluate what aligns to your interests, skills, and personality. Write down the occupations that are a match based on your research.

You have now explored three different aspects of what can make up your career path.

1. You have a list of your skills, interests, and personality traits due to your assessment exploration.

2. You have a list of your career ideas that you determined from your brainstorming sessions.

3. You have a list of occupations that interest you.

These three areas converge to formulate a focused career that you have found through your own exploration. Figure 4 shows that the three areas you explored now have some commonalities as is highlighted in gray. This is where these come together to provide you with a path forward. A printable version of this diagram is available for free on www.losstoboss.com. Print it off and fill it in. At this point, you may or may not have a clear path, but if you do, awesome. If you do not, that is okay. You now have more information about yourself and what path you might want to head down than you did before. Self-exploration is about the journey and the steps toward realization.

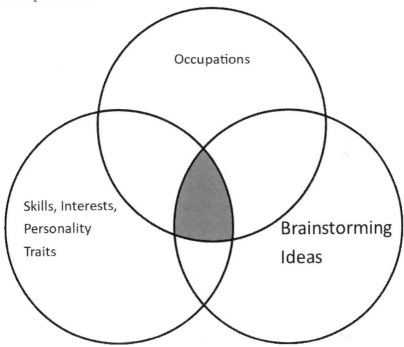

Figure 4.

You can now begin to formulate your thoughts, options, and research into some decisions. If you have completed all the steps up until this point, and you have a lot of great information about yourself. This information converges to point to one area, but you may be unsure of how to parse though all this information in order to come to a decision. It can be overwhelming and scary. With a lot of the heavy lifting out of the way, the next part can be a little more fun.

My recommendation is to utilize the following matrix in Figure 5. A printable version of this matrix is available on www.losstoboss.com. Take everything you have learned and begin to populate it with your options in order to draw conclusions on decisions. This tool will help you to begin to make sense of where you get more "yeses" and will help you to identify the top job occupations for you. Some of the things you write down on the left side such as values, skills etc., might be more important to you than others. Take that into consideration when you are making your decisions.

Write your job options (occupations) across the top and the list of your interests, skills, values, top brainstorm ideas, and continue with anything else that is important to you in a job. Then fill in the boxes with the different job options that meet those categories. They could either meet (yes), not meet (no), or maybe meet (maybe). In Figure 5, I've written in yes, no, and maybe to give you an idea of how to fill out the matrix. In your matrix you will have all of the boxes filled in with your answers. The job options will be specific to your exploration and your categories will be specific to you.

	Job Option 1	Job Option 2	Job Option 3
Interests (List your interests)	Yes		
Skills/Abilities (List your skills and abilities)	No		
Personality (List your personality alignments)		Maybe	
My Values (List your values)			
Top Brainstorm Ideas (List out your top brainstorm ideas on a separate line)			
Other things that are important to you			

Figure 5.

If this matrix does not work for you, you can always create a simple pros and cons list of each of the jobs you are looking to explore. This can help you to make decisions about what you want to pursue.

You have put in some work here. In the beginning of this book, I started by saying you must put in work to get work. If you have followed all the steps up until this point, you have.

If you are interested in narrowing down your job interests to get more granular but are having trouble deciding, you can try a guided visualization exercise. The exercise is about visualizing your different options to feel what option might be best for you. If you want to pursue something like this, you can utilize the free guided visualization exercise I have on my website. You can find it at http://www.losstoboss.com.

Step 4 - Company List

At this point you have a good understanding of the industry that might align to your skills, interests, personality, brainstorming, and potential occupations. You are off to a great start by moving up that flight of stairs one step at a time.

"Great things are done by a series of small things brought together" – Vincent Van Gogh [6]

The next step is to take what you have learned so far and begin to look at potential employers or organizations you may want to work for.

If you are not sure what companies are out there a good way to find a list is to do a web search for Fortune 500 companies. If you are interested in companies within certain states, you can always narrow that search down by typing in the state as well. For example, "Fortune 500 companies in Connecticut". This will give you a great list to get started from.

Other ways to find preferred companies might be to do a web search for "top companies to work for in Connecticut."

If you are interested in government jobs, it does not hurt to check out http://www.usa.gov to see the departments that might interest you. If you are interested in working at a nonprofit, a quick search for "top nonprofits in the US" will yield some good results.

If any of the searches I mentioned are not the types of companies you are interested in, that is ok. Simple web searches can begin to identify the companies that stand out to you as places you want to work.

In addition to the above, I recommend creating a dream company list. This is a list of ten companies you want to work for. Rank them in order starting with one being your most preferred company. By dream companies, I mean the companies that answer the question, "If I could work for any company I want, what company would I work for?"

Write down your list from one to ten, with one being the company you want to work for the most and ten being the company you'd least prefer working for. It is okay if you cannot come up with ten; the number of companies does not matter as much as doing the exercise so you can visualize the companies you want to work for.

This list is also beneficial, as it is not always about seeing what job openings are out there. One job search perspective is to identify the company you want to work for and pursue a job that they either have open or one that you solicit directly with them. Either way, it is important to have an idea of the companies that interest you.

Chapter 6

Develop Your Personal Marketing Materials

As a job seeker, you will need a certain set of personal marketing materials. This is how you promote yourself to potential employers. I am sure you are already familiar with the basics such as a resume, cover letter, and references.

I am going to run you through how to put these together in the best way possible.

Personal Marketing Material Strategy #1

<u>Resume</u>

A resume is an especially important part of your marketing materials. It is going to tell your story in a written format. It is a summary of your work experience and qualifications that align to the job you are applying to. There are many aspects of a great resume. I am not going to be able to cover them all here, but I will give you some of the basics. If after reading through this, you still need help, there are plenty of online resources to help you with either writing or editing. You can also hire someone to help you edit and write your resume. If your plan is to hire someone be sure to hire someone who is reputable and has references.

Be sure your resume is not just a list of jobs you have held in the past by date. You must think of it as a marketing tool that gives you another opportunity to promote yourself. It needs to say the things you want it to say.

This first part will talk about the different types of resumes there are, such as chronological, functional, and a hybrid of both.

The chronological resume lists your work experience in reverse chronological order starting with your most recent job. This is a preferred format for recruiters as it makes it easy for the person reading it to quickly run through it to see if you have the necessary experience required for the position. If you have a good work history without gaps, this might be the best format to go with. If you do have gaps, are changing careers, or are just starting out, you may want to see if one of the other resume types might be a better fit for you.

The functional resume organizes your work by highlighting your skills and accomplishments. If you have some great skills and accomplishments but not as much experience, highlighting each of your skills may help to bring out your top qualities. It can also highlight the skills you think are specifically pertinent to the position you are applying for. For career changers, showing off the skills you have gained through your career that coincide with your new career can really help you.

The hybrid resume takes qualities from both the chronological and the functional resume. You have sections with heading such as relevant skills and summaries. Parts of it will encapsulate your previous jobs along with a listing of your experience in reverse chronological order. If you are a career changer, this resume style is even better than functional as it shows recruiters your work experience while also highlighting your transferable skills.

You are going to want to highlight your skills in your resume as this is what employers are looking for in candidates. To determine what skills you may have, think about high level categories for skills important in a job setting. Examples include technical, management, project management, finance, marketing, people, or communication. These broad categories can help steer you toward the skills you have based on your life and work experiences.

Let's look at a list of skills that fall into those categories.

Computer and Technical	<ul><li>Technical writing</li><li>Video creation</li><li>Blogging</li><li>Information Security</li><li>Database Management</li><li>Web Design</li><li>Coding/Programming</li><li>IT Service Management</li><li>Network Engineering</li><li>Software</li></ul>

Finance	<ul><li>Accounting</li><li>Budgeting</li><li>Financial Management</li><li>General Ledger</li><li>Profit and Loss</li><li>Reconciliation</li></ul>
Communication	<ul><li>Verbal Communication</li><li>Written Communication</li><li>Teaching</li><li>Active Listening</li><li>Constructive Feedback</li><li>Articulate</li><li>Public Speaking</li><li>Presentation Skills</li></ul>

People	<ul><li>Patience</li><li>Positive Attitude</li><li>Diplomacy</li><li>Empathy</li></ul>
Personal	<ul><li>Integrity</li><li>Team Player</li><li>Creative</li><li>Willingness to Learn</li><li>Problem Solver</li><li>Dependable</li><li>Adaptable</li></ul>

This is not even close to an all-inclusive list, so it is okay to think of your own high-level categories and skills that would support them. Think in terms of what skills you have and where they align.

Now that we have reviewed the types of resumes there are, you may have an idea of which one you want to use.

There are hundreds of ways to lay out your resume and how you do that is really a matter of preference and depends on the industry you are looking to find employment in. An example of a resume that aligns to the industry would be, for example, if you are applying for a job in marketing or graphic design. Your resume may have a different feel as the creation of that resume and the design factors you may put into it could be part of your interview. It might be a little more creative and utilize aspects that are not typical in say a resume for someone in IT.

In Figure 6 I have included a standard resume format that has some extremely specific areas that we will go through.

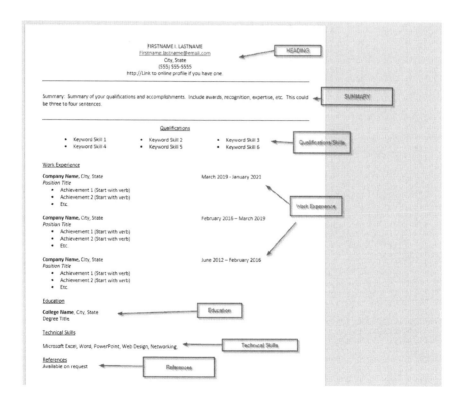

Figure 6.

Heading

The heading is where you write down your name, email address, the city and state where you live, the best phone number at which to reach you, and if you have any type of web link. Do not put your entire address in your heading as it is not needed; the city and state where you live is plenty to give the recruiter a geographical sense of where you are located. Some examples of web links I have seen are addresses to someone's LinkedIn profile, or a candidate's own personal website that promote themselves. This is a good place to include a link like that, but it is not necessary to have one.

Summary

The summary section of this example is where you would summarize yourself as a candidate based on your experience and education. It is just a few sentences outlining your qualifications for the position you are applying for. You should have a generic resume that has a general overview of your background to use if someone asks for your resume so they can float it around to people on your behalf, but when applying for specific jobs you will want to customize this section to be specific to that role. Do not make the mistake of generalizing when you are applying for specific jobs.

Qualifications

In the qualifications section of your resume, you will want to outline skills and qualifications that you have that are specific to the job you are applying to. These help a recruiter discern your skills quickly when looking over your resume. Also, this section is important for optimizing your resume for applicant tracking systems (ATS) which we will discuss a little later.

Work Experience

Your work experience should be listed in reverse chronological order starting with the most recent job you held. Each job should list the company name, where they are located (city, state), the dates of your employment, your job title, and your achievements or roles.

Your work experience shows your potential employer what you have done in the past and you will want to align that experience to the position you are applying for.

When you are listing your work experience accomplishments start each sentence with an action verb. For example, instead of writing "I was in charge of a $1,000,000 budget", you would write "Administered a budget of $1,000,000". If you are unsure what other action verbs you can use, a quick web search for resume verb lists will yield quite a few results that you can use as a plug and play word list to start off your sentences. Be sure each sentence you write has the proper punctuation.

Education

In this section of your resume, highlight your education. You will want to list the schools you attended and what degree type you received starting with the most recent. If you are still pursuing a degree and have not yet finished, you can write "Expected date of graduation: <date>".

You can also include other types of education you have completed. These may not be specific degree programs but other training or different types of education you have.

Technical Skills

The technical skills part of your resume may not even exist. What I mean by that is, depending on the type of job you are going for, this may not even be needed. If it pertains to the role you are trying to obtain, include it. This is where you would list any technical or computer skills you may have such as, MS Word, HTML, MS Excel. There are many other technical and computer skills to write in this section. You know what you are skilled in and should feel free wtp include those. If you have knowledge in these areas and it works in your favor to include them for the job you are applying to, then please do so.

References

Typically, references are not included on or with your resume unless the job posting specifically says to include your references. Most resumes at this point just say "references are available upon request." Usually, an employer will ask for your references the further along you are in the interview process, but again, if they are asked for up front, include them on a separate page. References are discussed further, later in this book.

The resume examples I have provided are not set in stone, meaning you do not need all of these sections and they absolutely do not need to be in the order I provided them. If you do not have as much work experience but have a degree that you are immensely proud of, move your education more toward the top. Do not stop there, whatever sections of your resume you feel are the best part of you and what you bring to the table, move them towards the top so they will be more prominent for the employer to focus on. Be sure to check your resume for grammar and punctuation. It is critical to make a great first impression and grammar and punctation can be a distraction from that goal.

If you are still not quite clear on how to write out your resume, I recommend either doing some web searches to gather additional information, get assistance from someone you know, or hire a professional. If you are going to hire a professional, be sure to do your homework and find someone who is reputable.

Personal Marketing Material Strategy #2

Applicant Tracking System

You may not have heard about Applicant Tracking System (ATS) software at this point, but it is an important program to be familiar with. ATS is a type of software that recruiters and companies use to collect, sort, and scan your resume and rank the applications they receive. This helps an employer to intake a large quantity of applications, and identify the ones that they most want to interview. The system does this by taking your resume's content and placing it into categories. Then it scans for keywords that are defined by the company to be specific to the job you are posting for.

In Jim's experience he found it very helpful to know and learn about Applicant Tracking Systems (ATS) for resumes

Jim was the VP of Audit and Control for an IT services company. Jim's role was to create the Audit & Control department from the ground up. He was responsible for implementing the requirements, processes, and tools to evaluate the company's management of customer projects, which included the financials, deliverables, and customer satisfaction. He oversaw all projects that had greater than $50K in revenue to help develop quality proposals and statements of work that were technically sound, properly estimated, and priced to meet profit objectives. In addition, he reviewed all long-term projects, led the closing out of projects, and changed and worked on at risk requests.

He had been with the company for a little more than three and a half years when it was purchased by a larger IT company. Everything was status quo for approximately a year and a half after the purchase. Then changes started. Staff were merged, and responsibilities and even management structure began to change. At this point, after 5 years with the company Jim's separation occurred.

Jim said that late on a Friday evening he received a meeting notice for 10am Monday morning from the COO for himself and his team. He was a little suspicious right off the bat since he had not heard anything about the meeting and did not know the purpose. Also, having been a Project Executive at a previous company, he was aware of a process where usually at the end of each quarter employees would receive a meeting invite late Friday evening for a meeting Sunday night with no details or agenda. It was a separation meeting for managers to prepare for upcoming separations. Managers would get the list early the next day so they could meet with the employee and contact the employee's customers effected by the separations to discuss the plan going forward.

First thing Monday morning, Jim went in to talk to the COO to get the details of the meeting. The COO said he was not supposed to discuss the details of the meeting but after some discussion, they let him know what was happening. At the 10am meeting, the COO and head of local HR to let them all know they were being separated from the company. They also provided the details about severance and forms that were needed to be reviewed and signed. Obviously, everyone was shocked. His team was a small but remarkably busy and integral group in their division. The reason for the separation was that the company did not feel there was a need for an Audit & Control department and were looking to trim costs due to missed financial targets for the poor prior year and quarter.

After the initial shock of hearing that he was losing his job for the first time ever, where it was not his choice to be able to leave on his own terms, he says he actually felt relief. Most of the management structure from the original company that he had worked with for five years was gone. His department had become very busy and was required to pick up more responsibility and was being forced into some of the new company's services policies. At that point, he realized that over the past months, a large amount of stress was building up with the current responsibilities. Reflecting on what had happened, it felt like they were not progressing in a good way functionality wise. Aside from shock, Jim progressed through all the stages of grief rather quickly to the point that, on his ride home, he accepted it and realized that this would be a good move for him.

After getting home and speaking to his wife again, he started to talk about what to do for a new job. His wife was a big support structure for him and even suggested that he take the summer off. He recognized after this suggestion that he had worked in IT for 27 years at that point, always working long hours. This included periods of working weekends and being on call with very few vacations where he did not have to work at least a few hours each day during his time off. The thought of having some time with no work responsibilities sounded kind of nice.

The biggest thing he missed from losing his job was not seeing the friends he had made while working there during those five years. He says while there was a lot of work, he did it alongside some great people who he missed. On the positive side, his period of no work responsibilities allowed for more time with family. He drove his youngest daughter to school each morning and took care of the new dog they had recently acquired. He was also able to spend a couple extra days with his older daughter. He drove her to college and over to her medical school interview one day. He helped her move out of her apartment and even took in a Mets baseball game just before college graduation. He and his family also took an extended trip to Ireland that would not have been possible if he were still working at his previous job.

He also went back to being more involved in a non-profit charity that he was previously involved in from which he had to step down due to job commitments and time requirements. He was the race director for a 5K race and one mile walk that had up to 1,700 participants and that raised more than $100K. Once he lost his job he returned and is now back with the race committee to help others.

During his time in between positions Jim kept up on his requirements for the certifications he held and recommends investigating the requirements and common certifications of jobs you are interested in pursuing. He says if you see a common mandatory or desired requirement, investigate getting those credentials.

When Jim did decide to return to the workforce, he monitored job boards and LinkedIn to see what was available. He hooked up with a couple of recruiters, but it did not yield any results for him. He ensured his resume complied with ATS recommendations. ATS was something he hadn't heard about up until that point. He feels as though having an ATS compliant resume allowed him to get more interviews than he would have without it.

He was able to land a position in IT Services but for the first time since entering the workforce he is not working for an IT company. He is working on the business side for a government employer as a Project Manager.

There have been some positives and some negatives to the new position. His new job has much better hours and less stress which is especially important to him now. He is no longer responsible for employees working for him and is now in an individual contributor role. He has also been allowed to explore other job responsibilities such as data and business analysis due to the lack of personnel available to perform those jobs for the project he is working on.

On the downside he has a much smaller salary, less vacation time, and less flexibility and influence over what can be done technology wise. The agency he is working for was a huge step down in technology advancement. He explained that it is almost like starting over for him in the technology industry. He is hopeful though that it will provide room to influence future technology improvements for the agency. Also, he sees a need to advance the project management methodology, role, and practice while there as it appears to be severely lacking.

Jim's recommendations for those that find themselves in job loss is to not panic. Knowing that he and his family were in a good place financially and that he did not have to rush into a job he may not like just to get money flowing back into the house was a big help. He recommends taking a couple of days to think about what you really want to do and not to rush into things. Put a plan together for how to look for a new job and who to work with.

A couple of lessons he wanted to pass on that he learned while going through this process is to have a professional review your resume. He says that he believes a resume is the first impression to the hiring staff and an underwhelming one can keep you from getting interviews. The review is not that expensive and well worth it. One thing he said he would do differently next time is to not schedule two interviews in one day. He said it made things feel rushed when he needed to be relaxed and in a good state of mind for interviews.

Another hint Jim found is that if you file for unemployment, he was required to go through a resume review and a meeting to help with the job search. He recommends you closely review the resume that is sent back to you from the Department of Labor (DOL), especially if you are in the IT industry. The changes made to his resume by the DOL resulted in several errors, including general spelling mistakes. He feels as though mistakes like this would make you look unprofessional to hiring managers as the resume is your first impression.

Again, his best advice when dealing with job loss is to take a deep breath and take a couple of days to think about what you genuinely want to do employment wise going forward. Do not rush into the process, and stick to the goals you set for yourself. Do not take a job just to get a job and start making money again. He said if you take a job that you are miserable in, you will just be looking for a job again soon.

Jim was able to leverage his ATS compliant resume to get more interviews. You can leverage it to help you in this way too. In simple terms the Applicant Tracking Systems removes the least qualified candidates from the stack based on logistics the employer has determined. What does this mean for you exactly? It means not only do you have to write a resume that conforms to all of the other things we already talked about, but you must also write and format it with the ATS standards in mind. Out of all the resumes a company receives, only about 2% of the applicants are contacted for an interview, so you must rise to the top of the stack to get scheduled for an interview.

ATS specifications to keep in mind: [15]

1. File type

    o   You are going to want to submit the proper file type for your resume. Do not use PDF as they are not the most compatible with ATS unless specifically asked to do so. Plain text files are very compatible with ATS but unfortunately have minimal formatting options. For the most ATS friendly, you will want to submit a word document which are files with the extensions .doc.

2. Headers and Footers

   o Do not use a header or footer on your resume for important information. The ATS system has difficultly identifying information in headers and footers, so keep the good stuff out of there, such as contact information. When I say header in this case, I do not mean the heading that we already discussed earlier.

3. Keywords

   o Keywords are an especially important part of ATS and how it works. The system is basically scanning your resume to find keywords that are pertinent to the position you are applying for, so you must make sure you have those keywords in your resume in the right places (placement) and in the right frequency (the number of times they appear).

   o To find the right key words, search for three to five job descriptions that are the same as the job you are posting for.

      ▪ Find the most used words or phrases across the different job descriptions.

      ▪ Place the same keywords in your resume in the following places.

         • In the qualifications section of your resume in the bulleted list which is toward the top of your resume

- Throughout your education and work experience section.

These are some of the ways to ensure your resume has a shot with an applicant tracking system. If any of the above seems confusing or you are not sure how to proceed, I would recommend you hire a professional who can help you through this part of the process.

Personal Marketing Material Strategy #3

<u>Cover Letters</u>

A cover letter is an important piece of your marketing material. It is a one-page document that is sent with your resume to provide additional details on your achievements. It can show your potential employer your personality and why you and the skills you bring to the table would be a good fit for their company. Just like any of your other marketing materials it will help recruiters to screen you for the job. A cover letter is like your introduction to your new potential employer. It is as if you are about to go on stage and the master of ceremonies (MC) is giving you this great introduction to pump up the audience for your appearance. The show is your resume for them to review first before you are on stage during your interview. Your cover letter should be unique to each position you are applying for. Stay away from canned cover letters, this is your opportunity to showcase your skills that are specific to this position. Sending a standard one does you a disservice. Take the time to outline each letter so you can put your best foot forward every time.

Now that the purpose of cover letters has been explained, let's talk about what goes in one and a template that you can use to create them.

The basic structure of any letter, including a cover letter, includes a heading, salutation, introduction, a body, and a conclusion, which is shown in Figure 7 on the next page.

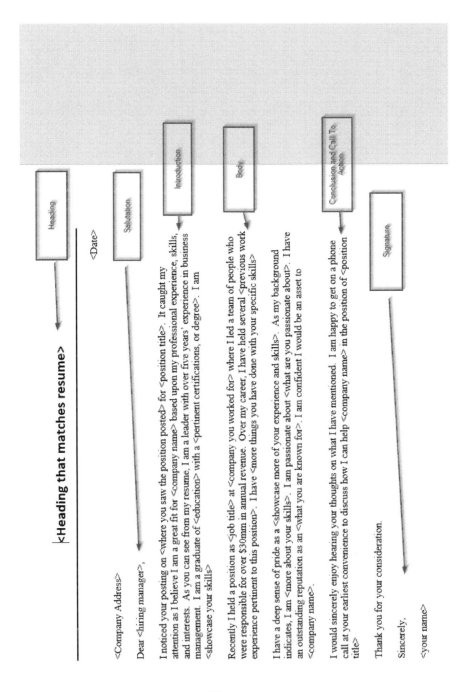

Figure 7.

Heading

This heading should be the same as your resume heading. There is no need to change that, as you have already put time and effort into creating it, and it's great to have matching pieces of marketing material.

Salutation

The salutation is the opening or greeting of the letter. You can keep it simple by using Dear to start off, but who do you address it to? I feel this is a key part to a cover letter. As with the other aspects of our marketing material, stay away from the generic salutation of Dear Sir/Madam. You should be using the hiring manager, or HR person's name. We are lucky to live during a time where most information can be found on the internet. Try to find this information by whatever means necessary. It may come to you through a web search or quite possibly someone in your network may know the person in the company who is doing the hiring. The point is, try to be as specific as possible and go more generic only if you need to.

Introduction

The introduction is meant to grab the reader's attention- in this case, the hiring manager or the recruiter. Use it to explain how or where you came across the job posting. If someone referred you, mention it. Introduce yourself and why you want the job.

Body

In the body of the letter, you will want to include at least two paragraphs outlining your education, skills, and work experience that is specifically relevant to the position you are applying to. This is where the bulk of your writing will go. Explain why the skills and qualifications you have will help your future employer.

Conclusion and Call to Action

You then want to finish up the letter reiterating your top strengths, as well as how the recruiter or hiring manager can contact you. This should be a call to action, not just information on how they can reach you. Make it more along the lines of: "I am happy to get on a phone call at your earliest convenience to discuss how I can help <company name> in the position of <position title>" [11]

Closing/Signature

This is where you put your closing salutation such as "Sincerely" or "Regards" followed by four blank lines and then your name typed out. The blank lines are enough space for you to sign your name.

The example I provided is only one option in a sea of others. There are a ton of examples out there on the web if you are looking for more options. As in the other areas I have discussed, you can also hire a professional to write a cover letter for you which may take any of the guesswork out of it.

Personal Marketing Material Strategy #4

References

You must have references when applying for jobs. Employers want to find out if what you are telling them is true. Ultimately, they want to know if you are effective and can handle the job, and they believe your references can provide them with that. In addition, a reference can be valuable to an employer as it can help to find out if you are a good fit for the company.

Keep your references on a separate sheet from your resume. See figure 8 for an example reference sheet. When you are working through the job process, references are typically asked for the further you progress through the process and are not usually asked for up front, but they could be. Some employers don't even want to waste time interviewing people until they've checked your references.

You will want to have a list of at least three references and no more than four unless specifically asked for a certain number. You will want to choose the right people to be references on your behalf.

\<Heading that matches resume\>

\<Date\>

References

\<Reference 1 Name\>
\<Reference 1 Job Title if Applicable\>
\<Reference 1 Company Name if Applicable\>
\<Reference 1 Address\>
\<Reference 1 Phone Number\>
\<Reference 1 Email Address\>

\<Reference 2 Name\>
\<Reference 2 Job Title if Applicable\>
\<Reference 2 Company Name if Applicable\>
\<Reference 2 Address\>
\<Reference 2 Phone Number\>
\<Reference 2 Email Address\>

\<Reference 3 Name\>
\<Reference 3 Job Title if Applicable\>
\<Reference 3 Company Name if Applicable\>
\<Reference 3 Address\>
\<Reference 3 Phone Number\>
\<Reference 3 Email Address\>

\<Reference 4 Name\>
\<Reference 4 Job Title if Applicable\>
\<Reference 4 Company Name if Applicable\>
\<Reference 4 Address\>
\<Reference 4 Phone Number\>
\<Reference 4 Email Address\>

Figure 8.

For ideas on who to put on your reference list, you can look to colleagues from previous positions, people you have worked with in the past, previous managers, professors, and former employers.

Choosing the right references is important. You will want people who can handle themselves well and can speak to different aspects of your strengths, skills, and aptitude. You will want references who you know and trust, and who know you well.

The number one rule of putting anyone down on your reference list is to ask first. Always ask your potential reference if they would mind being a reference for you prior to writing them down on your list. Also, if you are applying for positions and you have passed their name along, be sure to give them a heads up that they may be receiving an email or a phone call so they can keep an eye out. This might give them some time to formulate their ideas if someone reaches out to them about you.

References are a critical part of the job application process and as such it is important to choose wisely. References will validate what you have been telling your potential employer in your cover letter, resume, and interview, and can help to differentiate you from other candidates.

Chapter 7

Utilizing Your Personal Marketing Material

It is time to find your next opportunity and you are thinking about what options you have. There are many avenues to a job. In this chapter I am going to present to you six hot places to begin your search to increase your chances of finding your next job or new career. Let us run through some of these in order to give you an idea on how you can leverage them and what to expect.

Job Search Opportunity #1

Headhunters and Recruiters

Headhunters and recruiters do some similar tasks but they operate in different ways. They are both interested in finding talent to fill positions for companies, but each have a different perspective.

Recruiters typically work for and represent one company within a human resources department or talent acquisition department. They are responsible for sourcing and finding people to fill positions within the company they work for. They usually own the process from beginning to end including sourcing, screening, setting up interviews, making offers, and working through onboarding the person to the company.

When you see a job posting for a company, it was typically posted by a recruiter working for that company.

A headhunter will perform a similar role but work for either a third-party organization or themselves. Their job is to source and find talent for other organizations. They will help to coordinate interviews and offers and are usually in the picture up until the candidate receives a job offer. Working with a headhunter can really help you to find a job that will suit you, but be sure that a headhunter is not charging you for their services. Do not work with a headhunter that expects you to pay them for helping you find a job. Reputable headhunters are paid commission by the company they find talent for.

Job Search Opportunity #2

<u>Company Specific Job Listings</u>

If you are looking for a position at a specific company, you can check their website for openings. This is a good way to see what they have available. Typically, you can find a company's job openings by going to their website and looking for a link that says careers or jobs. If you do not see it at the top of the page, check the links in the footer that might say careers or jobs.

Job Search Opportunity #3

<u>Job Boards</u>

Job boards are another way to find jobs in your industry or by job title. There are quite a few out there and there are some benefits to using them such as:

- Job notifications that match your search criteria
- Many job listings all in one place

- A search capability that allows you to use specific criteria such as location, keywords, job titles, pay, education, experience, etc
- Saved profiles to help you to apply to job opportunities easier.
- There are even niche boards out there that are specific to certain job types. These niche sites can be specific to say construction, nonprofits, tech, etc.

Job boards can be a useful tool in the job search process. Check out some of the larger ones such as Monster, Indeed, and ZipRecruiter to get an idea of what they can offer you in your search. Try doing some searches to find jobs that are interesting to you.

Job Search Opportunity #4

Job Fairs

A job fair is an event where employers and recruiters are there to give job seekers information on their organization in the hopes of recruiting people for their open positions or to collect resumes. Typically, the fair is held at a venue where there are many tables set up by individual companies. As a job seeker you walk from table to table talking to recruiters from each organization. What is nice about an event like this is that you can go to one place and find out about many different organizations and what they have to offer. Some of these events even have on site interviews happening so that the process can progress quickly. It also allows you to network with potential employers and introduce yourself to multiple companies all at one time. [12]

To prepare for a job fairs, the first thing you will want to do is research who will be there. Now you can prepare for all the introductions you will have. Bring your marketing materials with you and make sure you have at least 20 resumes printed and ready to hand out. Dress as if you were going to an interview because first impressions count. Do not be shy; you must be willing to go up to recruiters and speak to them. This is your chance to show off your personality. Be sure to have your elevator speech ready to go for when you are meeting the recruiter for the first time. Put in some extra time and come up with a couple of different elevator speeches depending on what companies you plan on approaching during the job fair. When you do approach a recruiter, put your resume in their hand right away when meeting them, so you can refer to it as you are having your conversation. Prepare questions, so you can learn more about the type of organization you may be applying to. Keep in mind that before you leave the booth you need to ask for their business card. It will be difficult to remember each one you meet, and you will want to send a thank you note within 24-48 hours of meeting them.

For the companies you are interested in, follow the recruiters' instructions afterward and apply formally for any positions that caught your attention. This will probably include submitting your resume online as well. As you send out the thank you notes within the time frame of 24-48 hours, be sure to apply to the job within this time frame as well so you are fresh in their mind when they see your application come across.

Use these job fairs to network and get your name out there. They will help you to understand the opportunities that are around you. They will also open your mind to careers you may have never thought of before. Do a web search for job fairs in your area and plan to attend.

Job Search Opportunity #5

Networking

Networking with family, friends, and colleagues can help set you up with a hot tip or even a recommendation. Your network is a powerful thing. In fact, some of the best jobs I have had came from friends who pointed me in the right direction. Them pointing me in the right direction was even followed up with a recommendation, which went a long way in me getting hired. The fact of the matter is, sometimes it is who you know, not what you know, that gets you the job. Put your message out there to your network and let them know you are open to work opportunities.

Job Search Opportunity #6

Social Media Marketing

With social media today it is much easier to reach out to your network to see what might be available for you. LinkedIn is a great platform to connect with colleagues and business acquaintances. These connections and connections of connections can help you to track down the job you are looking for.

If you have a limited, family, friend, and colleague network, you can also look for networking events in your area. The types of networking events that you should look for are:

- College or university lectures: Colleges bring in industry experts and leaders for a networking event. These can help you to meet people in your field.

- Roundtable events: Where lectures combine an open forum for discussion.

- Industry specific speaking engagements: Learn from others in your industry. It can spark new ideas and help you to rub elbows with people who have the same work interests as you do.

- Happy hour meet ups: Geared to be more casual where a group of people can make small talk and meet others. I put this last on the list as this is not my first recommendation for someone out of work and currently looking for a new job as it may be a little too informal.

These networking events are a great way to meet people who are in your field while also learning new things. With the way technology works today, most of these events can be attended virtually which makes it possible to network with people from across the world while sitting right at home.

Tony credits his network with helping him through a situation when he was faced with losing his job.

Tony was a Network Operations Center Manager who was responsible for support 24 hours a day, 7 days a week, 365 days a year. The company he worked for was a communications company that provided business class internet service. His job included helping to repair and maintain large internet circuits to keep businesses' networks operational.

It was known by the employees at the time that the company seemed to be in trouble, but everyone was keeping their fingers crossed that it could be saved. It was apparent that the company had run into some financial difficulties. It was not until the very end that a company meeting was held with the entire staff when they knew for sure the company was being sold to another company out of state and people were going to be without jobs.

Everyone felt shock and denial right from the start. No one believed it was going to happen, but it did, and it affected about fifty employees including Tony. Anger had sunk into the entire group as they blamed the company for letting it get to that point. They felt as though the company was mismanaged which led them all to the situation they were now faced with.

It was a challenge to begin the job search right away as a condition of their severance, required them to stay with the company until there could be a transition to collect. That did not stop Tony. He was more concerned with being able to land on his feet, so he immediately started to look for a new job. The crippling feeling, he felt when finding out about his job outlook was not depression, but was fear. Fear that he would not be able to provide for his family. The unknown weighed heavily on his mind, but he pushed on.

It took about six months, but he eventually accepted what was happening. It turns out that the fellow employees who were all experiencing the same thing banded together to lean on each other and network. Tony believes it was this comradery that helped him get through the situation. They supported each other through it all; when one person had a lead or prospect, they would share it with the group or recommend one of the group members for the position.

Tony took the opportunity to level up his own game by working extremely hard on improving his communication skills, as well as by taking some self-help courses that were available. He continues to recommend obtaining as much training in your line of work, as investing in yourself is valuable. He was able to take inventory of himself and recognize what his strengths and weaknesses were. He worked toward eliminating as many of the weaknesses as possible, or taught himself how to work around them.

He also took the opportunity to spend more time with family, especially his grandkids. It taught him that there needed to be balance between work and life. He has worked to maintain that balance ever since.

Tony believes resumes, cover letters, and references are key to job searching. If you do not have the skills to create these yourself, he recommends finding a friend or even hiring someone to help. Tony also says learning interviewing techniques is key to helping you to stand out during an interview.

For his job search he utilized a combination of web sites and newspaper searches, but the most effective was networking. That is how Tony was eventually able to secure his next career move in the same field as a technician in a Network Operations Center. It was through his network of fellow colleagues who were also without a job that led him to the position. The new position had him starting at the bottom again, but through perseverance he was eventually able to acquire a management position. This experience allowed him to work with some very dedicated professionals that helped him to become a better manager and person. He learned to see the bigger picture and also learned more about the overall business than he had ever thought possible.

Tony's advice for someone who has lost their job is that while it is a traumatic experience, learn all you can from it, recognize the states of what you will go through and deal with, and remember that what you are feeling is normal. Remember that this is not your fault, and you should not blame yourself. Work through it as best you can and do not be afraid to involve other people to help. Utilize all the resources that are available to you. Network whenever you can which includes networking online through platforms such as LinkedIn. During his experience he stayed positive and focused and recommends others do the same as you will get through this.

At this point you have heard about people who have experienced job loss and the act of finding another job. There is a lot of wisdom in their stories which can provide a sketch of a roadmap for you to follow. They have outlined what worked and even the pitfalls; take their knowledge and run with it. What they have gone through and accomplished is not beyond what you can do. You can and will succeed where they have also. Keep moving forward and think positive!

Chapter 8

Job Interview Preparation

I have interviewed and hired hundreds of people for positions within the organizations I have worked for. I have interviewed many college students for internships and been on the decision committee for a lot of those hires as well. I have done many mock interviews for friends, family, as well as colleagues when I co-founded a mock interview group within a company I worked for. The purpose of the group was to help employees who were looking to change jobs within our company. Sometimes people want to try something new in the same organization but are not sure about going on an interview and getting their resume together. The group provided resume feedback as well as mock interview sessions to help them feel more comfortable with applying for other positions within the organization.

With interviewing and helping others with job searches, I have reviewed hundreds of resumes and cover letters, and provided feedback to many people.

<u>Interview Preparation</u>

Being prepared for your interview can help to alleviate stress and anxiety. When you have things mapped out and you are prepared, you will be much more relaxed and confident which is key to an interview.

Before anything else, preparation is the key to success – Alexander Graham Bell [7]

The Interview Process

There are multiple definitions in the Merriam Webster dictionary for interview:

1. A formal consultation usually to evaluate qualifications (as of a prospective student or employee).
2. A meeting at which information is obtained (as by a reporter, television commentator, or pollster) from a person.
3. A formal meeting with someone who is being considered for a job or position.
4. To question or talk with (someone) in order to get information or learn about the person.

On the surface this is a great definition of "interview", but it does not quite give the real purpose of a job interview.

The part of the definition that is extremely accurate is that it can help the interviewer gain knowledge from the interviewee. What it leaves out is that as an interviewee, you are also an interviewer. A job interview is more of a mutual exchange. It is not only the interviewer gaining knowledge, but you as an interviewee are also gaining knowledge about the company you are interviewing for. Keep that in mind that what makes a great interview is an exchange of information and not one that is one sided.

Given that, there are specific objectives of the interview which can include the following:

Employer Objectives:
- Evaluate the candidate's personality traits, skills, and abilities as it relates to the position.
- Gain an understanding of the candidate's strengths and weakness.

- Gather additional information that is not mentioned specifically or to add on to what is already in the candidate's resume.
- Help the employer make a more informed decision about continuing on in the process of hiring you.
- Give the employer an idea if you would fit in with the company culture

Candidate Objectives:

- Gain an understanding of the company culture.
- Gain additional knowledge about the organization.
- Gather more information about the job that was not in the job description.
- Learn about the people who work at the company and how they handle themselves.

How to Prepare for a Job Interview

Step 1- Pre-Interview Research

Researching the organization or company you are going to interview with is a key factor in preparing for your interview. Knowing about the organization you are interviewing for will help you to identify relevant questions to ask during the interview and will allow you to mix your newfound knowledge into your question responses when appropriate.

It is important to demonstrate your knowledge of the organization as it will give the interviewer the impression that you are really interested in working for them. An interview can be challenging when the interviewer asks a question about their company such as "What is something about our company that excites you or makes you want to work here?", and you do not have enough knowledge about what they do to be able to answer it. "What do you know about our company?" is an easy question to answer if you did your homework.

Now that we know why you should do your research before the interview, let's talk about how you go about doing that. There are many avenues for doing your detective work.

1. With social networks, your best bet may be to find a colleague who works there already and reach out to them to get a personal perspective on the company.

2. That leads us to number two: check out the company's website. Doing this will help you to get a really good idea of what the company does. Most sites have an "about us" page, and in addition, there is always a conglomerate of information to understand what they are in business for. Maybe they even wrote their vision or mission statement.

3. Do a web search for the company and check the news. Do they have any new and exciting news they just shared? Did they just get more funding to take their company to the next level? Are they moving into a new market? Did they hire a new CEO? These are all things to keep an eye out for. If you can identify any of these types of attributes, take the next step and research them more. Learn about it so you can bring it up during the interview at the appropriate time.

4. Do a search online for employer reviews related to the company. They are usually remarkably interesting to read and can give you an idea of the culture and what employees there value.

5. Do a web search for the job title and position and read as much as you can about what it entails so you are prepared to speak to it.

6. Research what department the job falls under, or what are some of the key skills are required to do the job. This will help you talk intelligently about it with the interviewer when the time comes.

There are a ton of resources out there to do your research. Interviewers want you to display knowledge of the company that you are applying to, and if you do not it could be a deal breaker. It is an important part of the process, so don't skip this one.

Step 2- Preparing Your Elevator Speech

An elevator speech is a brief overview of your background and experience. The term elevator speech comes from this scenario, if you were in an elevator and someone in a position of power asked who you were, you would have a short time frame to tell them about your value until you reached the floor either you or they were getting off on. Typically, this time frame aligns to an elevator speech of about 60 seconds. I say you can stretch it to 90 if you must.

Your elevator speech will be used for a few different scenarios. One being when you are in your interview and you are asked, "Tell me about yourself." The other place it can be used is at job and career fairs when you are talking to those at the table or booth. Likewise, it can be used at networking events and used as a bio on your social media sites.

To design your elevator speech, you should take a few things into account: your skills, positivity, goals, and persuasion. You do not need to run through all your experience. Choose a few key highlights that are impactful. If it is a networking event, you may want to start off your speech with introducing yourself with your first name. "My name is ...." and then talk about your most recent role and an accomplishment that you are most proud of. Then talk about your historical experience that led you to where you are. Finish it off with something for the future such as what you are looking to do next and why you are interested in this position or if it is during a networking event you can talk about the type of position you are looking to land. Have your speech ready because you never know what person of power you may be in an elevator with.

Step 3- Knowing What Questions to Ask During an Interview

You are going to want to ask questions during your interview, so it is important to have prepared some in advance. Your questions should be related to the position you are applying for. They should show off your knowledge of the company as well. Be sure to ask well thought out questions to show that you are enthusiastic about the position. These questions must be valuable in helping you gather more information on deciding about working for this company in this position. You should ask these questions at the appropriate time during the interview agenda. It is typically towards the end of the session. It is okay to jot down notes during this time as you gather information the interviewer tells you.

Some examples of questions to ask are as follows;

- What are some of the qualities of someone who is successful in this position?
- What types of training programs are available?
- What does a typical day on the job look like for this position?
- Can you share any thoughts on a career path for this position?
- What are the company's plans for the future and how does that relate to this department?
- What do you like most about working for this organization?

Step 4- What to Bring on Your Interview

We have been talking about preparation, and putting together what you are going to bring on your interview is a key preparation point. The first thing to keep in mind is to bring confidence.

**Trust Yourself, You Know More Than You Think You Do.
- Benjamin Spock [8]**

Extra Resumes

Bring extra resumes printed on quality paper in case the interviewers do not have a copy. Also bring a few copies of your references and letters of recommendations. Do not forget a copy of the questions you prepared in advance. If you have any certifications, or awards that you received, it can be a good idea to bring copies of those with you in the event that you are asked about them. Business cards are also a great thing to have on hand to give out. You do not have to spend a lot of money on business cards. You can usually pick up a small run of them online for $10-$15. It is a simple inexpensive tool that can help you get your name out there.

Of course, you will bring your phone, but be sure the ringer is off, and is on silent. Be sure to bring paper and writing instruments to take notes. All these things should be carried in some type of well-organized folio or briefcase.

Present Yourself

You never get a second chance to make a first impression – Will Rogers [9]

The previous quote by Will Rogers has a certain truth to it and when it comes to interviews it is a key aspect of the process.

The impression you make with an employer during an interview directly affects the outcome as being a failure or a success.

First impressions and the impact of those first minutes in an interview can be critical. It may be difficult to right the ship after not making a positive first impression but do not get discouraged if you think it doesn't begin smoothly. Pushing through any small issues and overcoming challenges are what companies want to see. Being prepared can help you get the interview off to a great start and can stack the deck in your favor for a positive outcome.

Punctuality is important, so be on time. You should plan to arrive 10 minutes early to allow time to get prepared mentally. During this time, you should also be observing what is happening around you at the location.

When you arrive for your interview you are going to be evaluated on several things, and one of them will be your attire. It is important to wear appropriate attire based on the position you are interviewing for. Wearing a suit can be flexible enough for multiple situations. A suit with the coat on is very formal, but when you remove it, it can change the look to be less formal. You will want to understand the company you are looking to work for and see how they dress. One way to do that is to do some research by either asking someone you know who works there or drive by the company during shift change to see what people who work there are wearing. Anything you can do to gather more information about the company you are interviewing is beneficial.

As a failsafe, when you speak to someone in human resources to set up your interview you can always ask what the dress code is or just wear a matching suit, jacket, skirt. There are a few colors which are traditional for this attire and that is black, navy, or dark gray. Your shirt should be simple, such as white or neutral.

During your interview, the less distracting you are the better, so dress appropriately and don't be too flashy. Be conservative when given the option.

Along the lines of flashy you should also pay close attention to body piercings, jewelry, cosmetics, perfume, or cologne. Sometimes in these instances, less is more. Hygiene is also an important factor. Showing up well groomed, with your clothing clean, pressed, and polished will go a long way.

When traveling for an interview be sure to follow a top rule and pack everything you need for you interview in a carry-on bag. I do this with all my important things when traveling and it can make lost luggage almost a non-issue. If you do have to pack and travel, be sure to break out the iron before you head to your interview.

The Interview Agenda

Chances are the agenda for an interview will be as follows. It will start with the opportunity to give your elevator speech, and then the interviewer(s) will go into questions with the expectation that they leave time at the end for you to ask any questions you may have. The process for interviewing may include more than one interview round, so keep that in mind as that is a normal part of the process.

Interview Types

There are a few types of interviews that you should be aware of, so you are not surprised.

1. Recruiter Call – basically this is a call from a member of HR to screen you. Chances are they saw something in your resume, cover letter, or qualifications that they liked, and they want to get an idea if you should be brought in for an interview.
2. One on One Interview – chances are you made it through the recruiter call and you are now in an interview one on one with quite possibly the hiring manager.
3. One to Many Interview – you were brought in for an interview and now you are in a room with more than one interviewer. They will each take a turn asking you questions. Some of the ways these are run is that they have each person in the room ask a question one at a time and give you a chance to answer them, with follow-up questions happening after each question. Sometimes each interviewer will just ask all their questions during their turn, and then move on to the next person in the room until they have asked all their questions.

4. One to Many One-on-One Interviews – This is the scenario where they may schedule a few hours of your time and have your time planned to meet with key people one at a time. Either you will move from office to office, or you will stay in one room and the interviewers will funnel in and out.

Modes of Interviews

We live in a connected world so while historical interviews took place mostly in person, now people have expanded their worlds to include other media such as phone and video conference which we will cover here. I cover in person interviews much more in depth later.

Your interview process may start off with a phone interview. Phone interviews are convenient because you do not have to travel to where the interview is, but the challenge is the person on the other end cannot evaluate body language. Nonverbal communication makes up more than half of how we communicate and with a phone interview, you are missing some of that. When in a phone interview, be sure to speak in an upbeat manner and smile. While you may think a smile does not travel over a phone, it does. Choose your words carefully and vary your tone and pitch as you do not want to come across monotone.

Remember to take your time and do not interrupt the interviewer by being sure they are finished with what they are saying prior to you speaking. If you must use a cell phone be sure you are in a place with incredibly good service to minimize dropped calls. If you don't have the best service, it's okay to mention that to the interviewer and make plans in case the call gets disconnected such as asking "what number should I call you back at?"

Video conference is now an option for interviews and with the COVID 19 pandemic it has become more popular at times than in person interviews to ensure social distancing as much as possible.

They are convenient as you do not have to travel. Also, with the amount of remote working that companies are adopting, you may be interviewing with a company that is headquartered quite a distance away.

With a video call you should treat it the same way as you would an in-person interview but keep these other tips in mind. Find a quiet place in your home to attend the interview away from distractions and interruptions. Ensure you test your camera and audio prior to the actual interview so you do not run into any unexpected technical issues at the time of the main event. Test using the same video conferencing platform that the interviewer used to set up the interview to ensure it is installed properly on your device and works as expected. If at the time of your interview you have some technical issues, do not panic. Stay calm and work through trying to figure it out. I recommend you are connected through a stable internet connection and try to avoid using cell phones when possible. When you do your dry run you should evaluate how you look in the perspective of the camera. You will want to keep the camera at eye level and avoid the up or down shot. Try to keep the camera on the same screen where you will see the interviewer. This will help with keeping you looking at the interviewer while speaking and can help with maintaining eye contact over video. Another factor to consider is lighting. Lighting is especially important when on a video call because if it is too dark or the light is too bright it can give the interviewer an unnecessary distraction.

Being able to adapt to different modes of interviews and overcoming challenges that they present can show an interviewer some of your flexibility and skills. If the thought of a video conference interview makes you nervous, do not be. You will prepare for it and you will do a great job.

Handling Interview Questions

We have already talked about the importance of preparation. Handling your interview questions is no different. You must prepare by leveraging a few key strategies. You have already learned about the company you are going to interview with and have come up with some great questions to ask during your interview.

Chapter 9

Interview Questions

Now you will see some examples of the types of questions you might encounter. This is by no means a complete list. You should do a web search for sample interview questions if you want to prepare for even more than what is listed here. Remember questions will pertain to the position and industry, so keep that in mind when deciding what questions to prepare for.

Here is an example of a question that is related to the job being interviewed for. A colleague of mine who ran an IT Help Desk always asked her candidates, "Knowing that you will need to be able to explain over the phone how to complete tasks for callers, please explain to me in detail how to make a peanut butter and jelly sandwich". For my colleague, this question allowed her to gauge the person's ability to explain things to people without being able to show them. It helped her, over the years, to find candidates who were successful as Help Desk agents. Would you encounter that question if you were interviewing for a Vice President of Finance position? Absolutely not, but at times interviewers will ask you to think outside the box and your preparation will be key in adapting and overcoming those instances.

Remember to try and keep your answers to 60 - 90 seconds. A person's attention span is not very long, and an interviewer is trying to work on multiple things at once, so you may only get a short time to give an impactful answer. Eliminate the need to ramble with your answers. Remember that pausing before answering is okay and it is better to pause and think about your answer before speaking without a plan.

Types of Interview Questions

Standard Questions

Inevitably an interviewer is going to throw out some standard type of interview questions and you are going to want to be prepared for them. You are even going to want to answer them in a specific way.

Sample Question List:

- Tell me about yourself
- What motivates you?
- What are your strengths and/or weaknesses?
- How do you handle stress on the job?
- What do you know about our company?
- Why do you feel you will be successful here?
- What are you short- and long-term goals?

You may be wondering; how should you answer questions like this? You are going to want to show the interviewer how you and your life relates to the job and the expectations of you as an employee. You will want to bring those to the forefront and showcase yourself, your education, experience, and skills. If you are looking for a more detailed method, there is one out there called P.A.W.S.. Do a web search for P.A.W. S. interview questions to learn more.

Behavioral Based Interview Questions

Behavioral based interview questions are designed to gather information about your past performance. The premise is that your future performance will be like your past performance. These questions can be specific to skills and traits relevant to the position you are interviewing for. Personally, for me, behavioral based interview questions are in my toolbox when I interview people for positions. I find that I can tell a lot about a candidate in the way they answer. You will recognize these questions by the way they start out. The questions usually begin with terms such as, describe a situation, tell us about a time or give an example of....

Interviewers may or may not use this format of questions, but do not be tripped up if they do. As I mentioned, these are some of my go to questions. I can tell when candidates do not prepare for these types of interview questions because they will not know how to answer them and will just give basic answers without describing for me the situation or provide historical examples of their performance.

How to answer behavioral based interview questions:

I have always relied on the STAR method to provide answers. STAR is an acronym to help you remember how to lay out your answer. It stands for; S-Situation, T-Task, A-Action, R-Result.

S - First, you want to set the SCENE or SITUATION and give some of the details to illustrate your example.

T - Second, you want to describe what your TASK or responsibility is in the situation you outlined.

A - You then want to explain the ACTIONS you took.

R – Lastly, explain the outcome or RESULT of the actions you took.

It is a fairly simple process especially if you think about it like you are just outlining a story for the interviewer.

Here are some examples of behavioral based questions: [14]

- Describe a group project you worked on. What was your role and what did you achieve?
- Tell me about a time you went above and beyond your manager's expectations to get the job done.

- Give an example of an occasion when you used logic to solve a problem.
- Tell me about a time when you worked on multiple projects; how did you prioritize?
- Describe a situation when the person you were trying to help was disgruntled or upset about the situation; how did you handle it?

Example Answers

Question: Give an example of an occasion when you used logic to solve a problem.

Answer:

The Situation

Recently I was working on a project with some fellow colleagues. The computer system of one of my colleagues who was testing out scenarios suddenly stopped working. By stopped working, I mean the screen went blank.

The Task

We needed this computer to be able to run the test scenarios as it had all of our scripts saved on it.

The Action

I started to logically rule things out to see where the issue might lie. The first thing I checked was the monitor connections to and from the PC and the power cords which did not show any loose connections. I noticed that the PC was not powered on anymore, so I decided to check the power coming from the wall. I plugged a desk lamp into the same outlet that the surge protector was plugged into and found that the lamp was working. I then plugged the lamp into the surge protector that the PC was plugged into and found that the lamp did not power on. I swapped out the surge protector and we were able to power the PC back on.

The Result

As a result of the troubleshooting and restoration of the PC, my team and I were able to continue working on the project.

I separated out each of the STAR pieces in my example by a heading. Of course, when you are answering the question, you will not say the situation, the task, the action, and the result. You will just tell each of the parts as one whole story.

The overview I gave illustrates the situation for the interviewer, the task as hand, the actions I took that align to the question, and what happened. This gives the interviewer a 360-degree view of the situation and how you got the final result.

Remember to practice these questions as much as possible. It will help to build confidence and get you in a groove for answering these types of questions.

Negative Questions

Interviewers will ask negative questions to try and draw out your weaknesses or poor reactions to tough situations. Just as in all the other questions, you just need to prepare yourself for these.

Examples:

- Have you ever felt like you were missing a skill?
- Was there ever a time you had to admit you made a mistake? If so, how did you handle the situation?
- What is your biggest weakness?

Answering these can be tricky but not if you are prepared. Be honest and talk about real work-related events but stay away from anything that may be specific to the job you are applying for. Also, do not respond with the cliché answer of turning the weakness into a strength, for example, "I am too much of a perfectionist at times". A good interviewer has heard that answer a hundred times. So, tell the truth and be sure to always end the answer with what you are doing to overcome the weakness. For example, "I have a tough time with public speaking, but I joined Toastmasters.org, and have been working through projects to help me improve my abilities. Recently I even delivered a maid of honor speech in front of a room of people and people told me afterwards they really enjoyed it."

Situational or Hypothetical Questions

The last interview question type I will cover here are situational and hypotheticals. These are questions that are designed to show the interviewer how you would respond to different situations. Utilize your past experiences, education, abilities, etc. to answer these questions.

Examples:

- Tell me how you would manage a large workload.
- What if a coworker is not pulling their weight while working on a group project with you?
- How would you respond to an issue you discovered?
- How would you handle a disagreement with a superior?

Preparation for these questions have two aspects. The first is that you research the company and position, so you know how to align your answers. The second is to formulate your "YOU" stories, which I will cover next.

The fail safe, "YOU" Stories

Whenever I am helping someone prepare for an interview, the first thing I say is you need to come up with a bunch of "YOU" stories. You may be thinking, I have no idea what you are talking about. Well, let me explain. "YOU" stories are a collection of stories that you've already mapped out (prepared) beforehand and practiced. These "YOU" stories give you a library that you can pull from that will help you react to most questions that are thrown at you. It is impossible to foresee every question that is going to be asked of you during an interview. By compiling a list of "YOU" stories you create a library of flexible answers that can be adapted to almost any question. These stories are formulated using your extensive work experience, or if you do not have a long history of work, you can draw on your personal life, or educational experiences. To gather these "YOU" stories you should write down major happenings from your past experience. What are your major work accomplishments? What problems were you able to overcome in work and life? These are the topics for your "YOU" stories. Plan these "YOU" stories out and practice them.

These "YOU" stories will help you answer any of the types of questions outlined above, so start self-reflecting and telling your story!

More Than Just Questions and Answers

As we have covered, interviews are more than just running through questions and answers. There is also a nonverbal side to how you communicate with the interviewer. This includes body language, gestures, eye contact, posture, tone of voice and others. Ensure you take this into consideration while communicating.

Be sure to smile when appropriate during the interview. Even if you are on a phone interview, it is important to smile while on the phone. It makes a difference in the way your words come across.

Body language is important. Be sure to use good posture without slouching and sit comfortably. Other nonverbal queues such as leaning forward when you are saying something exciting to bring your point in and nodding at the appropriate times can be helpful.

Be sure to maintain eye contact with the interviewer. Not being able to show eye contact may cause the interviewer to question your sincerity and believe you are not confident.

Why did you leave your last job?

A question may come up from a potential employer about why you left your last job. Being as some of this book is about helping those who lost their job find a new one, your story may not be the most positive in this regard. Not to worry though. Begin your response with a positive statement about your previous place of employment. Be honest and keep the details to a minimum. Stay away from using the word "fired" if possible. You should focus your answer on what you were able to accomplish in that role and emphasize what you learned from the situation. Bring your answer back around as to what you can do in this new role if chosen. Always stay positive and never say anything negative about your former manager, team, company, or employer. [16]

Example Answers

If you were furloughed/laid off:

Unfortunately, my position was impacted due to a reorganization. Since then, I have evaluated myself in consideration of my next opportunity. I am excited about this position as it will allow me to utilize the experience and skills, I have gained previously in a way to bring <COMPANY XYZ> and myself, success.

If you were "fired" or let go:

Being separated was one of the best things that could have happened. Now I have an opportunity to explore positions that better suit my experience and skills like this position. Would you like to hear more about my skills?

Pro Tip: *Practice*

Once you have developed your answers to the questions you think will be asked along with your list of "YOU" stories, the next step is to practice them. Don't just read through your answers and know what to say, but to practice them out loud. Hear your words to see how they come across.

An excellent way to do this is through a mock interview. Ask a friend or family member, to run through questions with you. If you are planning to set up a mock interview, you should be formal about it and see if you can run through your plan for the day of the interview, including having your materials ready to do a dry run.

While a friend or family member is great to run through questions with, at times you may want to look to hire a professional coach. Sometimes having the feedback of someone with extensive experience and the ability to provide open and candid feedback can be greatly beneficial and can help you be more prepared for the interview. Either way, get out there and practice the scenarios out loud.

Don't practice until you get it right, practice until you can't get it wrong. – Harold Craxton [10]

Handling Moments of Silence

In general people do not care for silence and feel awkward when it happens. If you have ever heard someone speak or have spoken yourself, you have inevitably said the word "um". It is a filler word while we are thinking so we do not have that dreaded silence. Try to minimize your use of um as much as possible when on interviews and in life. Silence can happen during your interview, and it is okay. Remain calm, and do not panic. Silence is not a terrible thing, and chances are, the silence you are feeling is probably a lot shorter than you think. If it does seem to go too long, you can always ask if they need any other details on your answer, but do not just go on with your answer or nervous talk just to fill the space.

Salary Negotiation

Negotiations

Do not bring up the topic of salary unless the interviewer does first, with one exception. If you have already had your first interview, it went well, and they have brought you back for a second, then you should broach the subject of salary if they did not already. One way to do that is to ask when it would be appropriate to have a conversation about salary. This allows the prospective employer to start the process. If they are open to the discussion, you can start off with "If I am the candidate you decide to hire would you be able to give me an idea of what the salary range is for this position?" [17]

If they ask you any of the following questions, you will want to ensure you answer them carefully. Some answers can quickly put you into trouble.

- What did you make in your last position?
- How much are you expecting to make in this role?

In the art of negotiation, silence is king. It is in your best interest to hold off on being the first one to the table with an amount. You are going to want to keep your previous salary very private during this negotiation and try to hold out as much as possible. If you are looking for more information on how to negotiate, do some additional research online.

To answer the question about previous salary or expectations on salary for this role, don't!

Do not disclose the information they directly asked for. You should bring the conversation around to the position you are interviewing for with responses such as, :I would like to talk about the value I can bring instead of my current pay. I want this new position to be an increase in responsibility as well as compensation."

Never say sorry, and keep your comments and discussion positive. Stay away from negative words such as "no". Turn a negative into a positive. For example, instead of "No, $70,000 is not the salary I was looking for", you can rephase it to say, "I would be more comfortable at $80,000."

These are a couple of things you want to keep in mind during salary negotiation. If you are interested in learning more about negotiating salary, there are many resources out there that can help you take it from start to finish. Negotiating can be a challenge, but do not leave this one to chance. You will be sorry later on if it's not handled correctly up front.

Chapter 10

A Lasting Impression

Finishing Up the Interview

It is important to know what will occur before they select a candidate for the position. Will there be another interview with you? Do they have other people to interview? Ask the interviewer when you can expect to hear back from them about a decision or when you should follow-up on the interview. It is important to get an understanding of the timeline. Once again, reiterate your enthusiasm about the position.

Be sure to thank the interviewer(s) for interviewing you and for their time. Also, be sure to ask for their business card. You can use the information on their card to send them a thank you note later on.

Sending a Thank You

Be sure to send a thank you note within 48 hours of the interview session. An email is great to send right away but follow it up with a handwritten mailed note. [13]

Follow this formula for thank you notes:

Address the letter or note directly to the person who interviewed you. Thank them for meeting with you, tell them what you enjoyed about the interview. Put in a follow-up to the interview, such as something that came up during conversation. Put together a short analysis of the problem the interviewer mentioned and include it along with saying you would be happy to talk about it further if it is something they think would be valuable. Talk about how much the company looks like it would fit you well, and how excited you would be to work there. End it with a message saying that if there is anything else you could help with to please let you know. Sign it with a "best regards", "all the best", or a "sincerely" and your name.

The goal of the thank you note is to show the interviewer how much you appreciate their time and to help them envision you in the position.

Chapter 11

You Can Do It!

At this point, you know about my own experience in losing my job due to my position and entire department being eliminated. You know what I went through when it first happened, but let me explain more.

One mistake I made when it first happened was that I did not tell my family. I kept it a secret for three days. Looking back on it, I realize that was not the best choice because it is important to get as much support as you can during this time. I remember vividly making a conscious decision to not tell because I wanted to come up with a plan before having the conversation. The purpose behind that was I did not want them to have unnecessary worry and stress about any of the situation. Eventually I did say what was happening, but at that point I really had accepted the situation I was in and felt confident that I would be able to find another job. I am glad my confidence was still intact and that I felt strong enough to continue making steps toward my next opportunity.

Here are some additional details of how things played out for me. The company I worked for gave me 30 days' notice, with a severance package. Within those 30 days a couple things happened which really helped me out.

I decided that this was an opportunity for me to evaluate what it was I would want to do going forward and looked to align that to what I felt I was qualified to do. I did a lot of writing to help myself analyze the many facets of this. I wrote down goals, and things that made me excited about work. I dissected the things I was doing on a day-to-day basis that I really enjoyed and tried to focus my next opportunity around that.

After I had come up with some ideas, I immediately touched up some of the experience on my resume; I always make it a habit to keep my resume updated as it is much easier to add my accomplishments as I go instead of trying to remember them all at once. I added a new summary which aligned to my goals for my next endeavor. I added skills that were related and made sure those skills were mentioned in other parts of my resume (ATS optimization).

After I updated it, I had some of my colleagues give it a proofread to be sure I did not miss anything, even though I had gone over it a bunch of times. Of course, they gave me some great pointers which allowed me to modify my resume to make it even better.

I began to reach out to my network to get my resume out there and to line up some references. Even without me asking, people told me that they would be happy to be a reference for me, which I gratefully accepted. Word began to travel quickly as I put the word out, and people started to ask me for my resume so they could pass it around.

I looked online for open positions to see what aligned to my goals and aspirations and applied to specific opportunities. I did not start applying to everything I saw. I made sure I was very calculating in what I submitted my application for. I was extremely detailed in making sure I tweaked my resume and cover letter for each opportunity to highlight my skills specifically to what I was applying for. I was on a good track and making progress.

Even though I was blessed to be able to move into the confidence stage quickly through all of this and found myself pushing on, I am not going to lie. Everything was not all rainbows and unicorns. There were times when I wavered, but it was my friends and colleagues who helped me through it from a logical perspective. They kept me on track when I slipped. My friends and colleagues who had been through job loss before seemed to know exactly what

I was going through and provided me with what felt like all the right advice.

As I was navigating my way through the process, one of my good friends who found out about what happened to me, asked me if I would be interested in him floating my resume to some people he knew. I of course said yes and thanked him. It turns out that he reached out to his contacts right away to pass my resume along. He happened to pass it along to someone who knew the hiring manager of a company that had a couple of positions open.

A recruiter from that company called me for a screening which seemed to go very well. Afterwards I was asked to come on site for an in-person interview. At that point when I told my inner network what was happening, and they immediately said we needed to do a mock interview. I found a bunch of interview questions online and dug out my list of questions I had used during mock sessions before.

One thing I did to prepare was to write down answers to these questions and practice them. What I found to be the most important thing besides these answers was that I came up with a bunch of "me" stories which I describe in this book as "YOU" stories. I outlined stories about myself and my accomplishments that pertained to situational based interview questions. Each of my stories had different options and results of what was learned depending on what kind of question was asked. My answers were plug and play. By utilizing different perspectives of the story I could mix and match to highlight the skills most pertinent to the question.

I sat for some mock interviews with my network and it really helped me to become more confident in how I presented myself. I utilized all the feedback they provided me to hone my skills.

I felt as though I was prepared for the interview. While on site I met with the hiring manager for a brief time and then met one on one with the CTO and the SVP of Human Resources. Everyone was great. The interviews allowed me to showcase my skills and explain my perspectives on how I work and accomplish things. My stories really helped me to give real world examples of my successes. By telling these stories I was able to illustrate for my interviewers each situation and the outcome. I liked hearing about the things they were accomplishing as well, and started to picturing myself in that position and enjoying it.

The interview went well and shortly after that they made me an offer to join their company. We were able to come to terms on an offer which I felt was beneficial to both of us. They treated me extremely well in all areas of benefits, compensation, and experience. The leaders I reported to were great and helped me to grow and learn quite a bit.

While overall it was a challenging time for me, there were some very specific people who helped me through it. If you are reading this, I hope you know who you are. When I needed you the most you were there. Having people help me who had been through it before gave me confidence that I would get through it. They would reassure me that the way I was feeling was perfectly normal and that things will get better.

If you have found yourself without a job or are looking to advance your career, use this book to meet the challenge head on. If it is because of job loss, know that you will get through this. If it is because you are looking for a career change, know that it will happen. Overcoming these challenges can take time. Know that you will look back on this just like I and others have, and realize how much better off you are because of it.

After you meet your goals, utilize what you have learned to pay it forward and help the next person facing these challenges. They may not outwardly show it, but they too could use the help.

Stay positive, believe you can do it, remember the value you bring to the roles you are in, keep going, and you will get from loss to boss just as others have.

Epilogue

A Gift For You...

Thank you for reading this book. I hope you found it to be helpful, inspiring, and enjoyable. I want to share with you a free gift that I think is very beneficial when on a job hunt.

Did you know 18% of job candidates never negotiate salary when being hired? And only 37% always do? Job candidates that do negotiate are likely to start with a 7% higher average salary than those who don't.

To put that into perspective, if you didn't negotiate and were being hired for a job that pays $50,000, you would be missing out on more than $10,000 over three years.

If you compound that 7% higher starting salary over a 10 career, you would be missing out on over $40,000. On a 20-year career its over $90,000. Don't miss out on so much money. Make sure you negotiate!

As my GIFT to you...

I am sharing my Tips for Negotiating a

Higher Starting Salary.

To get *Tips for Negotiating a Higher Starting Salary* head on over to http://www.losstoboss.com/salarytips

Thanks and Acknowledgements

Thank you to my wife Kelli for the countless hours of proofreading and discussions. You and I make the best team.

Thank you to my Mom for a lifetime of love and always being my biggest promoter and fan.

A big thank you to Brian, Tony, Jim, Joe, and Mike who allowed me to interview them for this book. You have all breathed real life into these pages with your inspiring stories of overcoming setbacks in your career. Your contributions will allow others to know they are not alone and give them an understanding of how they too can overcome like you all did.

Thank you to Dr. Tom Denham for taking time out of his very busy schedule to write the foreword for this book. Your willingness to participate in such an impactful way is greatly appreciated.

Thank you to Kara DeMaio for designing the covers; you always come through with your amazing creativity.

Thank you to Chris Hallenbeck and Great Point Publishing for all the help in getting this book published. I always appreciate your friendship, partnership, and encouragement.

Thank you to all my family and friends. Some of you aren't living on this earth anymore but you have all helped shape me into who I am today. There isn't a day that goes by that I'm not grateful for knowing you.

About the Author

Author Frank DeMaio has nearly two decades of experience working in the corporate world as an IT leader and Certified Career Coach. He has conducted countless interviews of candidates ranging from college interns to upper-level executives. He's reviewed and critiqued resumes, held mock interviews to ready candidates for interviews, and has helped people in their job search.

His perspective was born of more than his corporate experience. It also includes his personal experience. After losing his job unexpectedly, he bounced back and landed not only a job but a career that inspires him daily. He now hopes to expand his reach and help job seekers worldwide do what he did with help from his book **Loss to Boss**.

END NOTES

1. "Do something today that your future self will thank you for." quotespedia.org, 9 November 2021. https://www.quotespedia.org/authors/s/sean-patrick-flanery/do-something-today-that-your-future-self-will-thank-you-for-sean-patrick-flanery/

2. "Our greatest glory is not in never falling, but in rising every time we fall." Brainyquote.com, 9 November 9, 2021. https://www.brainyquote.com/quotes/confucius_10 1164

3. "Your mind is powerful. When you fill it with positive thoughts your life will start to change." Quotefancy.com, 9 November 2021. https://quotefancy.com/quote/1705480/Buddha-Your-mind-is-a-powerful-thing-When-you-filter-it-with-positive-thoughts-your-life

4. "You can only become truly accomplished at something you love. Don't make money your goal. Instead, pursue the things you love doing, and then do them so well that people can't take their eyes off you." Challengeachieved.com, 9 November 2021. https://www.challengeachieved.com/quote/you-can-only-become-truly-accomplished-a-5caa42a29f79fd03c01c5001

5. "It takes courage to grow up and become who you really are." Brainyquote.com, 9 November 9, 2021. https://www.brainyquote.com/quotes/e_e_cummin gs_161593

6. "Great things are done by a series of small things brought together." Brainyquote.com, 9 November 9, 2021. https://www.brainyquote.com/quotes/vincent_van_gogh_120866

7. "Before anything else, preparation is the key to success." Brainyquote.com, 9 November 9, 2021. https://www.brainyquote.com/quotes/alexander_graham_bell_387728

8. "Trust yourself, you know more than you think you do." Brainyquote.com, 9 November 9, 2021. https://www.brainyquote.com/quotes/benjamin_spock_100344

9. "Will Rogers Quotes." Goodreads.com, 9 November 9, 2021. https://www.goodreads.com/quotes/7515235-you-never-get-a-second-chance-to-make-a-first

10. "Don't practice until you get it right. Practice until you can't get it wrong." Philosiblog.com, 9 November 9, 2021. https://philosiblog.com/2012/05/29/dont-practice-until-you-get-it-right-practice-until-you-cant-get-it-wrong/

11. "How to End a Cover Letter with a Call to Action – Jobscan". Jobscan.co, 9 November 9, 2021. https://www.jobscan.co/blog/how-to-end-a-cover-letter/ 9 June 2020

12. "Benefits of Attending A Job Fair Other Than Securing Employment." Nextstopcanada.ca, 9 November 2021. https://nextstopcanada.ca/benefits-job-fair-securing-employment/18 June 2018

13. "Job Interview Strategy Before, During & After."
unlv.edu, 9 November 9, 2021.
https://www.unlv.edu/sites/default/files/page_files
/27/QuickTip-InterviewStrategy.pdf

14. "47 behavioral interview questions from top tech companies
– 2021 Update."
Pathrise.com, 9 November 2021.
https://www.pathrise.com/guides/45-behavioral-
interview-questions/ 5 February 2021

15. "aplusresumes | finding employment, career coaching,
life...." 9 November 2021
https://aplusresumes.wordpress.com/

16. "How to Answer the "Why Were You Fired?" Interview
Question." Thebalancecareers.com, 9 November 2021.
https://www.thebalancecareers.com/why-were-you-
fired-job-interview-question-2061201
20 April 2020

17. "Internship and Career Center - Salary Negotiation."
Icc.ucdavis.edu, 9 November 9, 2021.
https://icc.ucdavis.edu/interview/salary-negotiation
29 May 2012

Made in the USA
Columbia, SC
28 November 2021

49898087R00072